Road Trip into a Future: A Southern California Journey, 1960s–1970s

Russell J. Dalton

Diego Garzia

Alexander H. Trechsel

Alex, Russ & Diego

Copyright © 2021 Russell J. Dalton, Diego Garzia, and Alexander H. Trechsel

Revised 2023

Photos by Russell J. Dalton
Irvine, California
All rights reserved.

ISBN: 9798745968068

CONTENTS

1	California Dreamin'	1
2	Cars, Guitars, and Surfin'	3
3	The Laurel Canyon Mystique	11
4	Ladies of the Canyon	25
5	The Beatles in LA	34
6	Pop Stars	43
7	The Second Generation	48
8	Motown Moves to LA	59
9	Beyond Rock n'Roll	67
	Sources/Author Info	

From

**"Adventures in Hollywood"
Collection on Amazon.com**

Russell J. Dalton, *Hollywood Road Trips:
Visiting Famous Movie Locations.*
Amazon/Kindle Direct, 2020.

Russell J. Dalton, *The Road to the Hollywood Red Carpet.*
Amazon/Kindle Direct, 2021.

Russell J. Dalton, Diego Garzia, and Alexander H. Trechsel,
Road Trip into Music: A Southern California Journey, 1960s-1970s
Amazon/Kindle Direct, 2021.

Russell J. Dalton, *On the Road to Warner Bros. Studio.*
Amazon/Kindle Direct, 2021.

Russell J. Dalton, *Star Trek Landing Party:
A Road Trip Through Southern California.*
Amazon/Kindle Direct, 2021.

All are available on Amazon.com

1. CALIFORNIA DREAMIN'

This book is about the music and music locales of Southern California in the 1960s and 1970s. We take you on a narrated road trip to the locations and events of the singers, musicians, and songwriters who created the special musical history of these two decades. You see where these artists lived and died, where they performed, and what made this a special time and place for music of various forms.

In many ways, the concept of Southern California is a mythical construct, often created by outsiders. Southern California evokes a lifestyle or a state of mind: surfing under sunny skies, palm trees, the smell of orange blossoms, pretty women with long flowing blond hair (preferably driving a convertible), hip young men (although the definition of what was hip was constantly changing), and every one sporting a suntan. Steve Martin's 1991 movie, "LA Story" is partly fiction and partly the reality of contemporary Los Angeles. It is required viewing for anyone new to LA.

The music groups and artists described here sometimes created and often reinforced this imagery, and to a degree lived this lifestyle. It was an image of California that existed throughout its modern history—a land of sunny opportunity. It brought the 49ers to search for gold in the later 1800s. It brought a surge of migrants from the East starting in the 1940s. When one of the author's parents moved to California from Massachusetts in 1941, they were awed by the beauty of the state, the attraction of the beaches and the Pacific Ocean, and the opportunities California possessed. The immigration inflow largely continues to this day as the region's population has grown to nearly 20 million.

The California mystique still exists to a degree, along with other realities of Southern California. Los Angeles is now a world city that attracts new residents in droves. Many people don't find the opportunities they expected from the imagery, but many do. Music tastes have also changed. For example, the carefree beachcomber life of early 1960s surfing music is much less a reality today. The music community that was drawn to Laurel Canyon in the 1960s because it was inexpensive and close to Sunset Blvd. lived in houses that have become multi-million-dollar mini-mansions. Mostly tourists go to the Troubadour or the old hangouts that still exist along the Sunset Strip.

To develop this book, we identified distinct sectors of Southern California's music in these two decades. Then we selected key groups or artists in each category. Our standard was that the artists had, with one exception, to be from Southern California or based in California during a significant part of these two decades. The collection discusses over 50 different groups or artists. How the groups formed, what path they followed to success, their interconnections, where they lived at key points in their life, and their musical legacy. Perhaps the best example is the chapter on the Laurel Canyon mystique that describes the rise and fall of *Crosby, Stills and Nash*, the *Doors*, and several other famous folk-rock groups of the early 1960s—all in a short chapter of 11 pages.

INTRODUCTION

We settled on several key musical areas over these two decades:

- Surfing rock (e.g., *The Beach Boys*)
- Folk-rock groups in 1960s Laurel Canyon (e.g., *Crosby, Stills, and Nash*)
- Women artists of Laurel Canyon (e.g., Joni Mitchell)
- *The Beatles* in LA
- Pop Stars (e.g., Sonny and Cher)
- Laurel Canyon's second-generation artists (e.g., *The Eagles*)
- Motown in Los Angeles (e.g., Diana Ross and the *Jackson 5*)

The book's content also differs from a traditional book. This is a combination of a scrapbook, photo album, and short narrative history of each group or artist. We produced the book in **full color** so that you can see where Joni Mitchell lived or where George Harrison wrote "Blue Jay Way". Virtually every page has a color photo or two. The book is in a large format (8x10) to present the photos in more detail and is convenient for reading on a tablet. The large format also lowers the high cost of color printing. We drew upon multiple sources and book-length studies of these artists, as well as our personal knowledge and recollections of the era.

Our goal is to share an entertaining, light-hearted road trip to some of the sights and homes of the musicians that provided the soundtrack for the 1960s-1970s. We cover many groups and many genres in brief "sound-bite" sized presentations. This provides the background for planning a road trip to famous locations if you come to LA. Or, to see the stories and color images in this book if you haven't made it to LA (yet).

And you are allowed to hum your favorite song from each artist as you read along, as we did as we wrote.

Russell Dalton

Diego Garzia

Alexander H. Trechsel

Our thanks to Ginny Dalton for assistance on the photography road trips and Tony Smith as our rock consultant, as well as Chris Davis and Hannah Yeunhee Kang for their technical assistance.

2. CARS, GUITARS, AND SURFIN'

The Pacific Ocean creates a Californian lifestyle composed of cars, guitars, and surfing. The 1959 film, *Gidget*, told the story of a young girl drawn to the beach and the boys who hung out there. It spawned a series of beach party movies with teen heartthrobs such as Frankie Avalon and Annette Funicello (from Mouseketeers fame). Surfing the waves in Malibu became synonymous with California's youth culture. With it came its own vocabulary of hodads, gremmies, groms, wipeout, Noah, tubular, gnarly, hang ten, and other slang.

California also was a center for automobile innovation in the postwar era as returning GIs bought cars and started to modify them for looks and speed. George Barris, Ed Roth, Boyd Coddington, Vic Edelbrock, and others became leading innovators in the California custom car world.

The third element was the soundtrack for this new California image. Surfers displayed their silent movies of surfing to fans around the Southland. As a soundtrack for these films, they played music built around a heavy guitar sound, preferably from the locally produced Fenders. This encouraged the formation of local surf bands in Manhattan Beach (*The Revelairs*), Hermosa Beach (*The Vibrants*), Redondo Beach (*The Bel-Airs*), Westchester (*The Crossfires*, later to become the folk-rock *Turtles*), and the rest of South Bay (*The Challengers*). The high point was the Rendezvous Ballroom on the Balboa Peninsula where all the best bands performed. This was an almost entirely home-grown music movement, with high school groups playing at school concerts, weekend dances at the park, or fraternal lodges. California surf music began.

Dick Dale

The "King of the Surf Guitar", Richard Anthony Monsour, was born in Massachusetts in 1947. His family moved to Southern California in 1954 when his father took a job with Hughes Aircraft. He began playing his guitar in local country-western bars where a hillbilly musician gave him the name "Dick Dale" because he thought it was a good name for a country singer.

In the late 1950s, the now-famous music promoter Art Laboe added Dale to his rock and roll concerts around the Southland, and Dale recorded various pop songs on his father's Del-Tone record label. This built up a large local following and set the stage for what came next. Dale moved south to Orange County to be closer to friends and opened a record shop across from the Rendezvous Ballroom on the Balboa Peninsula. There were many surfers among his patrons and they encouraged Dale to start surfing. It became his second passion.

In 1960, Dale began to organize surfer dances at the Rendezvous. In a few months, 3-4,000 people turned up for the weekend events. He performed with a band named after his father's record label, The Del-Tones. These events were the first stirrings of the surf music phenomenon.

At the end of 1961, Dale and the Del-Tones released an instrumental "Let's Go Trippin'" from their regular set at the Rendezvous. Many experts regard it as the first surf-rock instrumental. It launched the surf music craze and rose to #60 on the Billboard national chart.

Dale's instrumentals were distinctive because of his fearless guitar playing. He used unconventional chord combinations, a unique picking style, and amplifiers turned up to the maximum volume. Some claim his style was a precursor to the heavy metal bands that came later. The Rendezvous became a music and dance destination for youth across the Southland. One visitor was Clarence Leo Fender, found of Fender Electric Instruments in Orange County. Working together with Fender, Dale pushed the boundaries of electric amplification technology. Fender developed new equipment that produced previously unheard volumes; they also pioneered portable reverb equipment. A custom-made Fender Stratocaster, The Beast, became Dale's instrument of choice.

Dale released his first album, "Surfer's Choice", in 1962. This brought him national attention. He also drew on his middle Eastern heritage to transform a Greek folk song into the haunting "Miserlou" that he played during his 1963 appearance on The Ed Sullivan Show. (The song played over the opening credits of the 1994 movie, *Pulp Fiction*, which renewed interest in Dale's music). Dale named his second album in 1963 after his performing nickname, "King of the Surf Guitar."

A teenage Brian Wilson and his friends came to the Rendezvous in the early 1960s to hear Dale. They were blown away by his guitar skills and the energy of his music. A few years later, The *Beach Boys'* performed their first live show at the Rendezvous before Dick Dale took the stage. The *Beach Boys* later recoded two of Dale's songs, "Let's Go Trippin'" and "Miserlou", on their "Surfin' USA" album. (The Rendezvous was later destroyed in a fire, only a plaque on the boardwalk now notes its location.)

Dale's fortunes started to fade by the mid-1960s as other groups and other genres crowded the music scene. These other groups mixed the music style of Dale's instrumentals with catchy lyrics that appealed to young listeners. But Dale was there at the beginning of the surf culture and music in Southern California. He opened the doors for others. Dale later explained his style: "There was a tremendous amount of power I felt while surfing, and that feeling of power was simply transferred into my guitar".

Jan and Dean

Unlike most rock bands, *Jan and Dean* can trace their roots back to playing on the same football team at University High in West LA. After practice, a group of guys sang in the team showers because of the reverb effects. Soon they moved to Jan's music room at his Bel Air home. Besides sharing football and music, they both were auto enthusiasts. Jan Berry drove a new turquoise '57 Chevy Bel Air with a fuel-injected 327 engine. Dean Torrence drove a '32 Ford Deuce truck.

After graduation in 1957, Dean served a six-month stint in the U.S. Army Reserves. Jan meanwhile recorded a couple of records, one that burst onto the charts and went gold. Six months later, *Jan and Dean* reunited as a duo.

Their first record, "Baby Talk", didn't do well, so they hired two young managers: Lou Adler and Herb Alpert who would become key members of the LA music community. The managers arranged for the song to be played in an LA pop music station's new record contest. It won the first day, then the second, and then on for a week. This notoriety and rising sales got them a play on Dick Clark's *American Bandstand* where they also won the new song contest. Then a personal appearance on *AB*. They were off and running with their first record, reaching a #10 ranking on the Billboard chart.

They struggled to repeat this success for the next three years, with only one record reaching the top 50 on the Billboard chart. Then one day in 1962 they were driving to the beach in Dean's new Corvette and heard the *Beach Boys*' "Surfin'" on the car radio. It had a profound effect. J&D redid their style to adapt the harmonies and vocal doubling of the *Beach Boys*. They looked for a new song for their new style. In 1963, the *Beach Boys* were the opening act at a *Jan and Dean* concert. For the encore at the concert, Jan and Dean sang two *BB* songs and an ongoing relationship began between the two groups.

When Brian Wilson later attended a *J&D* recording session, he gave the duo a new song he had written about a fictional surf spot where there are "two girls for every boy." Dean and Wilson jointly revised the song and Brian joined them in the studio to record "Surf City". It became the first surfing song to earn a #1 ranking on the Billboard chart.

I bought a '30 Ford wagon and we call it a woodie
(Surf City, here we come)
You know it's not very cherry, it's an oldie but a goodie
(Surf City, here we come)
Well, it ain't got a back seat or a rear window
But it still gets me where I wanna go

The collaboration between the two groups continued. They went on several tours together. The older established *Jan and Dean*, and the youngster *Beach Boys* with two teenagers in the lineup, Carl and Dennis. Dean sang on the *Beach Boys'* "Barbara Ann"; Brian sang on *J&D*'s "Drag City". The record coauthorship continued even after both groups achieved national prominence. Dennis Wilson and Dean would race cars against each other at the San Fernando Drag Strip, and the two groups would sing at car shows at the LA Civic Arena or the Pomona Fairgrounds. It was a synergistic relationship.

Jan and Dean also sang about life in Southern California. "Dead Man's Curve" is about the bend in Sunset Blvd. just north of the UCLA campus; "The Little Old Lady (from Pasadena)" was based on a local auto dealer's ad featuring a senior citizen driving a Super Stock Dodge. Altogether, Jan and Dean reeled off a half dozen top-ten records in a row.

This ride came to a screeching end in April 1966. Jan crashed his Corvette on Whittier Drive in Beverly Hills, just 2 miles away from "Deadman's Curve". Berry received severe head injuries that required extensive rehabilitation. cooperation. When Jan recovered the duo began performing again. Although they never had another record break into the Billboard Top 100, they helped create the California beach mystique that endures until today.

The Beach Boys

Meanwhile, in the South Bay a group of teenagers was forming a band: the three Wilson brothers, with Brian Wilson as the singer-songwriter, their cousin Mike Love, and a school friend, Al Jardine. They lived in Hawthorne, a postwar suburb of Los Angeles and relatively close to the beach. Their little bungalow home (3701 W. 119th St.) sat where the I-105 freeway now runs, marked by a historic marker for their now-famous former home.

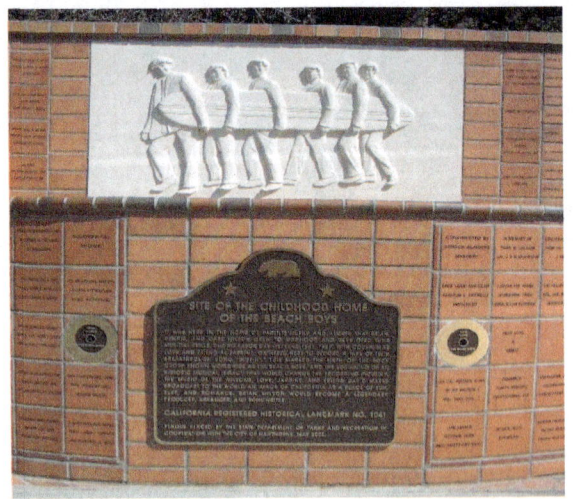

Brian had written a song for his high school piano harmony class. The traditionally oriented teacher gave him an F grade for "Surfin'". Brian persisted and borrowed a bit from Chuck Berry to revise the song. Their band played at school dances across the South Bay, covering the music of other popular bands. The Wilson band finally recorded a demo and found a record company that valued the new surfing genre. They wanted to call themselves the *Pendletones* to honor Dick Dale's *Deltones*. The record company changed the band's name and *The Beach Boys* were born with their first new single, "Surfin'" in December 1961. Appropriately, their first live performance was as the warmup band for Dick Dale at the Rendezvous Ballroom.

Their debut album, "Surfin' Safari" was released in October 1962 and rose to #32 on the national charts.

> *Let's go surfing now*
> *Everybody's learning how*
> *Come on on safari with me*
> *(Come on on safari with me)*
>
> *At Huntington and Malibu*
> *They're shooting the pier*
> *At Rincon they're walking the nose*
> *We're going on safari to the islands this year*
> *So if you're coming get ready to go*

The album catapulted them to the top of the charts and began an incredible run in music creativity. They recorded the next album, "Surfin' USA", in the famed Studio B at the iconic Capitol Records building in Hollywood. The band released three albums a year for three years straight. All but one was in the Billboard top 10 and all but one had gold record status. Brian Wilson became a creative force in Southern California music, writing for other bands including *Jan and Dean*, managing an all-girl group (*The Honeys*), producing records, and even singing with other groups.

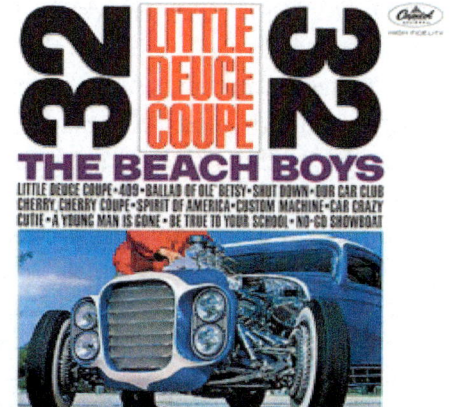

Beach Boys music offered evocative songs about the life of surfers and youth courtship on the California beaches, such as "Surfin' Safari", "Surfin' U.S.A.", and "Little Surfer Girl". The hidden irony was that Brian Wilson didn't surf and didn't like the ocean. His brother Dennis was the surfer in the family and tutored him on the beaches and surfer slang.

Their other preoccupation was California's adoration of hot rods and fast cars that generated songs like "409", "Shutdown", "Fun, Fun, Fun," "Little Deuce Coupe", and their first #1 single "I Get Around".

Intermixed with these songs were Brian Wilson's experiences as a young man. "Be True to Your School" was a callout to Hawthorne High School. Other songs dealt with youthful love, or love lost: "California Girls", "Help Me, Ronda", "Do You Wanna Dance?", and "Barbara Ann".

"In My Room" was a public acknowledgment of Brian's insecurity and mental struggles, compounded by a domineering father. His childhood bedroom in Hawthorne was an escape and sanctuary—away from the crowds, his father, and the challenges of his new life.

If you were a Southern California teenager in the early 1960s, you couldn't go cruising to the A&W on Hawthorne Blvd. or the Wich Stand on Slauson, take a date to Culver City's Studio Drive-in, or go to the beach without hearing the *Beach Boys* on the car radio. There was even an informal dress code: chino pants with a white t-shirt. If it was a dressy occasion, an open Pendleton flannel shirt.

The amazing thing was the national success of this new sound from an unknown group of kids. The *Beach Boys* reinforced the mystical image of life in California for the rest of America. Their music wasn't Mozart or Beethoven, but there was new creativity in their work. The *Beach Boy's* harmonies and compositions were innovative, especially when powered by the band's Fender guitars. Brian was also technically advanced in developing their instrumentation and recording methods. Most important, Brian's words captured the imaginations of American youth, and the purity of his voice spoke to their thoughts. At least in the 1960s, the *Beach Boys* sold more records than Mozart or Beethoven.

But then the world changed. On December 26, 1963, Capitol Records released the *Beatles* "I Want to Hold Your Hand" in the United States". Their new sound and European hipness rocketed them to the top of the charts and Capitol Records had a new star band. The *Beach Boys* began to worry that they were stuck in a rut, singing about surfing and cars. Brian is quoted as saying that the Beatles' "Rubber Soul" album "blows my mind" for its creativity. The *Beach Boys* even recorded three *Beatles* songs on their "Beach Boys Party" album.

Brian Wilson was AWOL, however. He stopped touring with the band in 1964 because of his anxieties; he was replaced by Glenn Campbell on the tour. Brian started smoking pot, and then acid. He wrote "California Girls" during an LSD trip at his new apartment at 7235 Hollywood Blvd.

His new drug-using friend, David Crosby, introduced Brian to the *Byrds* and their folk-rock style that would soon sweep through the American music scene. This set Brian on a path to create his masterwork. The *Byrds* opened for the *Beach Boys* at their Hollywood Bowl 1965 summer concert.

[Brian Wilson's Hollywood Apartment House]

Wilson moved to a new home at 1448 Laurel Way in Beverly Hills (1965-67). This is where he notoriously built a sandbox inside the house for his piano. That way he could compose while pretending to be on the beach.

[Brian Wilson's House on Laurel Way]

There he wrote his revolutionary *"Pet Sounds"* album that was released in May 1966. Instead of cute tunes, it was a life story told in Tony Asher's lyrics and Brian's musical innovations. Although it had modest sales success, some experts list it among the all-time greatest popular music albums. Paul McCartney said that "God Only Knows" was one of the best love songs ever written and the *Beach Boys'* greatest work:

> *I may not always love you*
> *But long as there are stars above you*
> *You never need to doubt it*
> *I'll make you so sure about it*
> *God only knows what I'd be without you*

The striking difference in lyrics from "Surfin' Safari" shows the band's evolution in four short years; the music changed even more. Lennon and McCartney were inspired by the album, which influenced their creation of the "Sgt. Pepper's Lonely Hearts Club Band" album.

"Good Vibrations" was released in the fall and was the last Brian Wilson authored song to rank at the top of the Billboard chart. Its series of four discrete musical movements created a pop music version of the classical sonata. Brian Wilson was continuing to grow as an artist.

The *Beach Boys* continued touring without Brian Wilson. Brian continued with his next masterwork "Smile" at his new home in Bel Air (10452 Bellagio Road, Bel Air). For the next several decades, however, Brian descended into a life of mental illness and drug addiction. A sorry tale. "Smile" was eventually canceled. The band released a series of singles over the next decade that never broke into the top 10 on Billboard. *Beach Boy* tours were mostly a look back to their past glory.

One day in 1968, Dennis Wilson picked up two young female hitchhikers and brought them to his house for a tryst. Soon after, Charles Manson showed up with a bus full of more young women and drugs. Manson gradually ingratiated himself with Dennis, who tried to get his producer, Terry Melcher, to offer a recording contract to Manson and The Family. The *Beach Boys* recorded one of Manson's songs, "Never Learn Not to Love" and released it on one of their singles in 1968. Their relationship soured, and Dennis leased a new house to escape from the Manson clan. In the early morning of August 9, 1969, members of The Family broke into Melcher's house to kill all the occupants. The house had been rented to Roman Polanski who was filming in Europe, Sharon Tate (Polanski's pregnant girlfriend) and five others were killed that night. The Family killed Mr./Mrs. LaBianca the following night in a random act of violence—writing "Helter Skelter" in blood on the refrigerator door. When the Manson Family went on trial in 1970, Dennis refused to testify.

In 1983, Dennis Wilson accidentally drowned in Marina del Rey next to his boat. Carl Wilson died of lung cancer in 1998. After his recovery, Brian finally released "Smile" in 2004 to less than critical acclaim. In September 2005, the Hollywood Bowl hosted Brian's performance of the 'lost' masterpiece "Smile" for his SoCal fans. It was an unusual but memorable concert. In 2012, Brian Wilson, Mike Love, Al Jardine, and others formed a 50th anniversary *Beach Boys* tour. It was a bit sad at times to watch Brian struggle on the concert stage. Still, their joint performance was a testament to the band's influence on American popular culture. Brian Wilson is one of the most influential pop music composers of the last 50 years.

* * *

Other California groups contributed to the surf music craze: *The Surfaris, The Challengers, The Hondells, The Honeys, The Rip Cord*s, and others. By the latter part of the 1960s, however, music tastes had moved on to folk-rock and then other genres. Still, a summer doesn't pass in Southern California without one or more beach towns hosting a surf music concert to celebrate the heady days of the 1960s. And it is easy to find yourself humming a *Beach Boys* song as you drive to the beach in the California summertime.

3. THE LAUREL CANYON MYSTIQUE

In the middle of the Aquarian decade of the 1960s, there were two centers for the music of a new American generation. One was Haight-Ashbury in San Francisco, with the flower children and acid rock music of the Fillmore. This was the land of the *Grateful Dead, Jefferson Airplane, Big Brother and the Holding Company, Janis Joplin, Creedence Clearwater Revival,* and *Country Joe and the Fish*. One of this book's authors visited there during the 1967 Summer of Love.

The other center was Laurel Canyon in Southern California. Laurel Canyon started at Crescent Heights near the end of Sunset Blvd. This is where Pandora's Box (formerly at 8118 Sunset) and the Whiskey a Go Go (8901 Sunset) took root, eventually accompanied by nearly two dozen other music venues on the Strip. This is where young Hollywood hung out, and groupies came to meet their idols. The kids from the valley and the beach came to cruise on Friday and Saturday nights. From there, it was a short drive or a hitchhike up to the canyon.

Laurel Canyon is a thin ribbon through the Hollywood Hills to the top of the mountains and Mulholland Drive, and then down the northern side into the San Fernando Valley. John Mayall was one of the first musicians to move into the Canyon. His 1968 song, "Laurel Canyon Home" captured the free spirit that defined life in the Canyon:

> *Each and every morning*
> *When the sun is high*
> *I hunt around the Canyon*
> *Till I find a place to lie*
>
> *Oh, oh, it's so beautiful to be alone*
> *Got the sun and trees and silence*
> *I'm in my Laurel Canyon home*

Halfway up the canyon is its touchstone—the Canyon Country Store (2108 Laurel Canyon Blvd.) This is where canyon residents came for essentials, where groupies came to stargaze, and stoners came for late-night munchies. The store is a central reference point for those traveling through the canyon.

In the late 1960s, the store's basement held the Café Galleria; it was a great place to end a night in Hollywood or hang out with Canyon residents. A favorite dessert was fruit sorbet served in the fruit shell. Then the Bistro became a British shop, and today it is the Laurel Canyon Cleaners and Laundry.

Mama Cass Elliot famously lived in the basement of the Canyon Country Store when she first came to Southern California. Some claim that this experience contributed to the lyrics of the *Mamas and Pappas'* "Twelve Thirty" which reflected the culture of the Canyon:

Young girls are coming to the Canyon
And in the morning I can see them walking
I can no longer keep my blinds down
And I can't keep myself from talking

Young girls and boys flocked to the Canyon for its alternative culture. A tradition evolved to have a community photo taken in front of the Store each summer. A tradition that continues.

The Canyon Country Store, Then and Now

When Jim Morrison and his girlfriend Pamela Courson moved to Hollywood in 1966, they rented an apartment behind the Canyon Country Store (8021 Rothdell Trail). They lived there while Morrison penned the lyrics to *The Doors* album "Waiting for the Sun." When their first album, "The Doors" was successfully released, they moved to another home.

Morrison wrote a poem called "Love Street" about their home; it became the basis of his song of the same title. Courson was the woman in the song, and Morrison wrote about sitting on their balcony and watching the stream of young people going to the Canyon Country Store.

I see you live on Love Street
There's this store where the creatures meet
Wonder what they do in there
Summer, Sunday, and a year

[Renovated Morrison House on Rothdell]

The Byrds

Morrison was attracted to the Canyon because of the music environment that already existed there. In early 1964, Jim (Roger) McGuinn was performing at the Troubadour club in Los Angeles. Gene Clark approached him about forming a duo to play *Beatles* covers. Then David Crosby, another regular at the Troubadour made it a trio. Chris Hillman joined the band in the fall. They became the house band at Ciro's Le Disc on the Sunset Strip which allowed them to develop their distinctive new style with their wondrous harmonies, unique guitar chords, and powerful songs. They first shared it with the glitterati of Hollywood. Then *The Byrds* released their first

[Gene Clark's House]

album, "Mr. Tambourine Man," in the summer of 1965; it transformed popular music and created the new genre of folk-rock. Their second album "Turn! Turn! Turn!" came out in December 1965 and rose to Billboard's top 20. Their remake of Pete Seeger's title song became their most successful single

In the Fall of 1964, Chris Hillman rented part of a house on Magnolia Drive with a panoramic view of LA. Hillman co-wrote the song "So You Want to Be a Rock 'n' Roll Star" at the house (which later burned down in a fire). Gene Clark, the group's singer and prolific songwriter, lived at (2018 Rossila Pl.; above). McGuinn and his electric 12-string Rickenbacker guitar lived in the Canyon. David Crosby lived at 8333 Lookout Mountain Ave. until moving to Beverly Glen (10422 Lisbon Ln.—where he was living when he was fired by his bandmates. Crosby was a frequent sight in the Canyon, roaring down the road on his motorcycle with a cape flowing behind him. Or one of the famous *Byrds* would stop at the Country Store.

The *Byrds* became "America's answer to the Beatles" because of the ethos of their songs, their harmonies, and McGuinn's art with his Rickenbaker. They had eight singles in the top 50 by March 1967. Yet by late 1967, the core band was gone after four albums. Clark had quit, and the band fired Crosby. Still, their records, five joint albums, and their presence in the Canyon were a foundation stone for Laurel Canyon's reputation as the musical home of the 1960s counter-culture.

[David Crosby's house in Beverly Glenn]

The Mamas and Papas

Early in their music career, John and Michelle Phillips were living in New York City. Michelle was a Californian who dreaded the eastern winters and longed to return to California. After one winter storm, her yearnings led John to write a song:

All the leaves are brown
And the sky is gray
I've been for a walk
On a winter's day
I'd be safe and warm
If I was in L.A.
California dreaming
On such a winter's day

Finally, in January 1965, John and Michelle Phillips drove from New York to California to revive their music career. Denny Doherty joined them on the cross-country trip. Once in Los Angeles, they reconnected with Cass Elliott who had been part of the *Mugwumps* with Denny. John came to LA with a set of songs that would define the California hippie feeling: "California Dreamin'," "Monday, Monday."

John and Michelle bought a simple one-bedroom one-bath home in Laurel Canyon on Lookout Mountain Road (8671 W Lookout Mountain Ave). The cover of their first album was taken in their Laurel Canyon bathroom

Within a year, the *Mamas and Pappas* were at the top of the charts and on the road to fame and fortune. Some say that the group's name was taken from Hells Angels' slang for men and women. In about three years, the group released five studio albums and 17 singles, six of which made the Billboard top ten.

John was a productive force beyond the *M&P*. He wrote the anthem of the 1960s: "If You Are Going to San Francisco (Wear a Flower in Your Hair)" that his friend, Scott McKenzie, made famous. Philips also organized the famous 1967 Monterey Pop Festival.

But internal drama arose with the band. Michelle Phillips had an affair with Denny

[John and Michele Philips House]

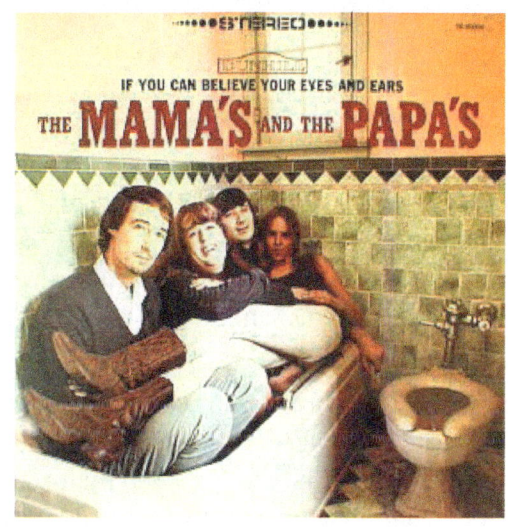

Doherty who lived nearby on Appian Way (8803). The offspring of this liaison was John's plaintive song "I Saw Her Again" in which he sings:

> *Every time I see that girl*
> *You know I want to lay down and die*
> *But I really need that girl*
> *Don't know why I'm livin' a lie*
> *It makes me want to cry*

It seemed that every young male in Southern California had a crush on Michele. Many of the early songs by John and Denny were aimed at Michelle. This was Laurel Canyon in the Sixties.

When Michelle began an affair with Gene Clark of *The Byrds*, John (who was not himself an innocent) kicked her out of the band for several months. She eventually rejoined the band, but the reformation was short-lived. The centrifugal forces of fame and fortune had moved them in different directions.

The Philips family left the Canyon and moved to a Bel Air estate (783 Bel Air Road) in 1968. John and Michelle divorced in 1970. Their joint California dream came to an end.

The Monkees

The Canyon was constantly adding and subtracting members of its community. As the Phillips left, a new band took up residence in the canyon. Columbia-Screen Gems created *The Monkees* for a TV series to draw upon the surging interest in rock bands. They created a band as the stars of the show, which came on the air in September 1966. The band's first single, "Last Train to Clarksville" sold a million records in the first month. *The Monkees* became a fixture on television and Laurel Canyon for the next several years. Even Carol King wrote songs for the TV show.

Micky Dolenz bought a home in Laurel Canyon (2441 Horse Shoe Canyon Rd.), just a short distance from the homes of Mama Cass and Frank Zappa. Instead of the single-focused hedonism of his past, he developed two activities. The first was hosting a seemingly endless stream of outrageous parties for his music and Hollywood friends. The second was building the house's recording studio to work on his music and for his guests. Brian Wilson once left his isolation at the time to jam with John Lennon. Dolenz still has the unreleased tapes.

Peter Tork of *The Monkees* bought a house just over the hill in Studio City (3615 Shady Oak Rd) at the end of a long, winding, and private driveway. Dolenz and Tork's homes were known for some of the most famous--and infamous—parties. Tork would venture down into Hollywood and hang out at Art's Delicatessen, Canter's, or a music venue on the Sunset Strip until the groupies arrived, and then head back to the Canyon.

[Micky Dolenz house]

Tork's house came with a pool that added an extra party feature—clothing was optional. The house also became a rehearsal venue after a young carpenter, Harrison Ford, built a music room. Crosby, Stills, and Nash did their pre-Woodstock rehearsals at Tork's house. Sooner or later, most of Laurel Canyon's music royalty partied or rehearsed there. Tork tired of the partying in the early 1970s and sold the house to Steven Stills and he moved into the basement of David Crosby's house. This was a tight-knit music community.

The Doors

The Doors were created in Venice, CA. It was close to the beach, cheap, and had good vibes. Jim Morrison lived with a friend and slept on the roof as he did drugs and wrote music (14 Westminster Ave., Venice). He connected with Ray Manzarek, a fellow UCLA film school student, and moved in with him and his girlfriend (at 147 Fraser Ave., Santa Monica). Manzarek's musical style was a key factor in *The Doors'* success. Adding Robby Krieger and John Densmore completed the band. It was during this period that Morrison wrote "Crystal Ship", "Soul Kitchen", "Break on Though", and "The End."

[Morrison's Rooftop in Venice]

The Doors became a house band for the Whiskey a Go Go in July 1966. They developed their style and Morrison grew into his shaman role, fed by LSD, pot, and alcohol. They recorded their first album for Electra Records at Sunset Sound and it was released in January 1967: "*The Doors*". Morrison was already dealing with his demons and the 12-minute finale of "The End" was his Oedipal exorcism:

This is the end, beautiful friend
This is the end, my only friend
The end of our elaborate plans
The end of ev'rything that stands
The end

[8632 Wonderland Ave]

The rest of the band joined Morrison in the Canyon. Manzarek lived in various houses. One later burned in a fire; the funky post-Doors house (8632 Wonderland Ave.) was his office and he shared it with his manager, Danny Sugarman. Sugarman wrote the tell-all book "Wonderland Avenue" about the crazy lifestyle of the era.

Krieger and Densmore lived at 8826 Lookout Mountain. Morrison was a frequent visitor. One day in 1967, Morrison was depressed and went for a walk to watch the sunset with a view of LA. He returned to the house with a set of written lyrics that became "People Are Strange".

People are strange when you're a stranger
Faces look ugly when you're alone
Women seem wicked when you're unwanted
Streets are uneven, when you're down
When you're strange . . .

Densmore later recounted Morrison's words: "*Yeah, I feel really good about this one… [His eyes were wild with excitement.] I scribbled it down as fast as I could. It felt great to be writing again*".

Morrison moved from the Canyon in 1968 and continued his life as a wanderer. He never bought a house for the rest of his life. He spent his time on tour, at friends' houses. When he was in LA, he often stayed in room 32 at the Alta Cienega Motel (1005 La Cienega Blvd.) near Pam Courson's apartment, the band's offices (8512 Santa Monica Blvd.), Barney's Beanery (8447 Santa Monica Blvd.), the Electra Records Studio (962 N. La Cienega), and several now-closed dive bars that Morrison frequented. His room has been preserved for Doors fans to stay in or visit for a fee.

[Robby Krieger and John Densmore House]

The "Light My Fire/The Crystal Ship" single rose to #1 on the charts. As the band prepared their next album, Morrison was in a downward spiral, challenging the boundaries of taste and the law. Their third album, "Waiting for the Sun" was their only album to top the sales charts at #1. The top single, "Hello, I Love You" was one of the last remaining songs from Morrison's creative days in 1965. One could see The End was coming for Morrison and the band.

The cover of their fourth album, "The Morrison Hotel", was taken at a hotel of the same name in downtown Los Angeles. The hotel has struggled over the years, closing and reopening. It is a poignant ending that the window on the album cover now graces a derelict building at 1246 S. Hope

[Morrison Hotel on Hope St.]

Morrison's last album was "L.A. Woman" in 1971. He died in Paris of a drug overdose 3 months later. He had written his own epitaph: "I see myself as a huge fiery comet, a shooting star. They'll never see anything like it again and they won't be able to forget me—ever".

Crosby, Stills, and Nash

In 1969, a new trio formed in the Canyon. David Crosby returned to LA after a self-exile to Florida after his expulsion from *The Byrds*. Steven Stills had been part of the *Buffalo Springfield*. He was an on/off resident of the Canyon at various houses including a house on Ridpath Dr. (8510) for a while, which has hosted many Canyon celebrities over the years. Graham Nash had been part of the Hollies. They connected through the Laurel Canyon network, evenings at the Troubadour, and hanging out with Mama Cass.

Graham Nash was living in Joni Mitchell's house on Lookout Canyon (see chapter 4). The house was a gathering spot in the Canyon because of its proximity to other artists. For example, *Canned Heat* lived next door and Frank Zappa was a few doors away. When David Crosby and Stephen Stills dropped by one night, their intricate harmonies intertwined, and *Crosby, Stills, and Nash* was born in that little house.

[Stills' House on Ridpath Dr.]

They released the debut album for their new band, "Crosby, Stills & Nash" in May 1969. Later that summer they made their memorable performance at Woodstock, cementing their place in rock history and continuing the legend of Laurel Canyon.

The Canyon was a magical place at a magical time. One day after returning from a shopping trip with Mitchell, Nash sat down and penned "Our House". Its lyrics and score are haunting. It is both a tribute to their relationship and one of the most memorable songs recorded by *CS&N*.

> *Our house is a very, very, very fine house*
> *With two cats in the yard*
> *Life used to be so hard*
> *Now everything is easy 'cause of you*

Their 1970 "Déjà Vu" album included the band's newest member, Neil Young. By that time, the foursome was already starting to splinter. The creative spark that had fueled the collaboration and creativity had faded. Nevertheless, some variants of *CSN&Y* collaborations irregularly toured over the next five decades, largely reliving the 1960s for those who were there, or who wished they had been.

Their 2005 album, "Crosby, Stills and Nash: Greatest Hits," is like a soundtrack for life in the 1960-1970s: "Our House", "Teach Your Children", "Marrakesh Express", "Carry On", "Long Time Gone", "Wooden Ships", "Guinevere", and others. Their two political anthems of the 1960s, "Ohio" and "Woodstock" weren't included.

Neil Young

The Canadian folk singer, Neil Young, relocated to California in 1965 in search of greener music pastures. He quickly connected to the Laurel Canyon/Troubadour network. *Buffalo Springfield* formed as a combination of Young, Richie Furay, Bruce Palmer, and Stephen Stills. Stills wrote their first hit, "For What It's Worth" released at the end of 1966. It referred to the Sunset Boulevard clashes between hippies and young people on the strip versus the police. As the Vietnam War expanded, it also became a standard of the anti-war movement.

> *There's something happening here*
> *But what it is ain't exactly clear*
> *There's a man with a gun over there*
> *Telling me I got to beware*
>
> *I think it's time we stop*
> *Children, what's that sound?*
> *Everybody look, what's going down?*

Buffalo Springfield dissolved in 1968. One of Young's traits was his ability to reinvent himself from band member to soloist, and from one genre to another. This gave him a long and varied recording career.

At Joni Mitchell's suggestion, he began his solo career with a record contract from Reprise. His first album, "Neil Young" had limited sales. Then he partnered with a band that renamed itself *Crazy Horse* and went on tour. In 1969, *Neil Young with Crazy Horse* released the album "Everybody Knows This Is Nowhere" which featured his songs and voice. It rose to #33 on the charts.

[Neil Young's home on Utica Dr.]

During part of this time, Young lived in Laurel Canyon at 8451 Utica Dr. The property looks like a Hobbit encampment. Young lived in one cabin and John Densmore lived in another. In 1968 Young moved west to Topanga Canyon, which was a more rural and rugged version of Laurel Canyon—far from the hustle and bustle of Hollywood. A few years later he traded Topanga for his Broken Arrow Ranch in Northern California.

In the summer of 1969, Young joined *Crosby, Stills, Nash, and Young*. He was with the band at Woodstock but didn't appear in the movie because the contract wasn't yet signed. The *CSN&Y* 1970 album raced to the top of the chart and was a huge success. However, Young and Stills were back to their old artistic battles from the *Springfield* days, and CSN lost the Y in 1970.

Young continued his largely solo career of varied styles and self-images, with periodic reunions with *Crazy Horse* and *CSN&Y*. He has produced over 40 albums and published over 1,000 songs. Young was nominated for an Oscar (for the song "Philadelphia"). Some of his most memorable songs date from the 1960s-1970s: "Heart of Gold", "Southern Man", and "Down by the River" and others.

Frank Zappa

Frank Zappa's infamous log cabin house was on the corner of Lookout Mountain and Laurel Canyon Blvd (2401 Laurel Canyon Blvd). It was movie star Tom Mix's home in the 1920s. In the early 1960s, it was inhabited by a free-flowing group of hippies, dancers, and members of various alternative movements. The huge living room in the three-story building hosted irregular concerts and dances. The bowling alley in the basement was a bonus attraction. Several of the more creative women of the house formed the *GTOs* (Girls Together Outrageously) that danced and promoted their unconventionality all over Hollywood.

Into this mix came Frank Zappa and his family in 1968. Zappa rented the house for his family and as a studio for the *Mothers of Invention* who rehearsed in the former bowling alley. Given his radical image, many people forget that Zappa made two appearances with the *Monkees* in a TV episode entitled "The Monkees Blow Their Minds".

Along with the building came the former residents. One of Zappa's projects was producing the *GTOs*, who continued to stay in the grotto on the property. The former renter and dance organizer lived in a room off the basement.

The partying on the property continued as Zappa tried to organize the *Mothers of Invention* as well as his other projects such as the album "Hot Rats". *Alice Cooper* was another project, and Zappa signed them to a recording contract.

The log cabin became a place to hang out, ranging from new groupies to old friends to famous stars coming to experience its environment. Zappa often locked himself away upstairs to work, while the partying occurred in the huge living room. Zappa also held auditions for his Straight and Bizarre record label, during the intervals between guests.

Eventually, the cabin's notoriety became too much, even for Frank Zappa. He, Gail, and Moon Unit Zappa moved to a larger and more isolated funky house at the top of the canyon (7885 Woodrow Wilson Drive). On Halloween in

1981, the log cabin burned down. Today it is still an empty lot but you can see remnants of the building and the grotto on the hill.

Even in these few months, the cabin created a new legacy for the Canyon. In 1968, John Mayall's album "Blues from Laurel Canyon" had the song "2401" (the address of the cabin) that paid homage to Zappa and the environment of his Laurel Canyon home.

There's a hero living at 2401 and all around
A family circus in the sun
Got his Mothers working
While you're having fun

Trying to change the system
Many things that must be done
Where did Moon go?
Better call a GTO

[Zappa Home on Woodrow Wilson Drive]

The *Mothers* broke up, and then were reborn. Zappa experimented in film making. He continued to produce records under the Bizarre and Straight record labels, then the two labels closed. He produced the album "Good Singin', Good Playin'" for the studio musicians known as *Grand Funk Railroad* in 1976. He was an innovator with music synthesizers. It seemed that creativity and chaos were standard features of his life, and the house on Wonderland became his respite. Zappa continued his energetic creativity at the Woodrow Wilson house until his death in 1993 from prostate cancer

In 2004, *The Rolling Stone Album Gui*de wrote: "Frank Zappa dabbled in virtually all kinds of music—and, whether guised as a satirical rocker, jazz-rock fusionist, guitar virtuoso, electronics wizard, or orchestral innovator, his eccentric genius was undeniable."

* * *

Many other bands lived in the Canyon or passed through it during the 1960s, along with individual artists on their way up or down. But it is the amalgamation of such talent in one place and one time that makes Laurel Canyon so exceptional. Some people compare the creative environment of Laurel Canyon to Florence during the Renaissance, fin-de-siècle Vienna, or Paris in the 1920s. Linda Ronstadt said it was like interwar Berlin. Laurel Canyon certainly had more rock and roll.

[Doug Weston's Troubadour pre-pandemic
9081 N Santa Monica Blvd, West Hollywood]

[Whisky a Go Go in 2021
8901 Sunset Blvd, West Hollywood]

4. LADIES OF THE CANYON

The 1960s were the time of rock music and rock music bands in Los Angeles, and most of these were all-male bands. The producers and record company officials were almost all male. Life in the Canyon was different, however. A counterpoint to the testosterone rock bands were the Ladies of the Canyon who expressed the new age with poetry and song. They often provided the cohesion that held together the fragile community of artists and egos, or at least provided bridges between different parts of the community.

Joni Mitchell

One lady perhaps best personifies these Ladies of the Canyon – Joni Mitchell. She had the look of the California hippie Earth goddess, even though she was born and raised in Saskatchewan, Canada. For a time, she performed in New York City and there connected with Judy Collins, Leonard Cohen, and other established artists. She met David Crosby while she was singing in a club in Coconut Beach, Florida. Crosby helped her develop her look and sound, and then they traveled together to Los Angeles in 1967.

Mitchell was already a successful songwriter. Her evocative "Both Sides Now", recorded by Judy Collins, was released in 1967. There was an autobiographical authenticity to many of Mitchell's songs, and this song was written at a time of tribulation for her.

I've looked at love from both sides now
From give and take and still somehow
It's love's illusions that I recall
I really don't know love
Really don't know love at all

In 1969, Collins won a Grammy for her version of" Both Sides Now".

Crosby produced Mitchell's first album, "Songs to a Seagull" in 1968 which received modest praise. She wrote from her heart about love, hardship, and her experiences in life. Her voice was mesmerizing and free of the heavy production used by other artists. Mitchell used the royalties from the album to buy a house in Laurel Canyon (8217 Lookout Mountain Ave.).

Mitchell's house is centrally located, just a few houses off of Laurel Canyon at the first stoplight beyond the Canyon Store. Her dining room overlooked Frank Zappa's duck pond next door. Because of its location and its owner, her house became a gathering place for the artistic community of the Canyon, especially after she and

[Joni Mitchell's House on Lookout Mountain Ave.]

Graham Nash started living together. She already knew her fellow Canadian, Stephen Stills, who lived in the Hollywood Hills. So it was fitting that the first harmonies of *Crosby, Stills, and Nash* occurred during a jam session in the living room of Mitchell's house.

The iconic picture of Mitchell looking out of a window was taken at the front window. The house is little changed today. It sits quietly by the side of the road, keeping the memories alive from that time.

Mitchell continued to make music history. In 1969 her second album, "Clouds" was released and earned her the first of nine Grammys. "Ladies of the Canyon" came out in 1970. Other artists were drawn to the poetry of her songs, from Judy Collins to Willie Nelson to Frank

Sinatra to the most famous example: Woodstock.

Mitchell was slated to sing at Woodstock. She was the opening act in the *Crosby, Stills, Nash, and Young* concert the day before in Chicago and traveled with them to New York City. Her Sunday appearance at Woodstock was canceled because of transportation problems. Instead, she sat in her hotel room and watched the television coverage. The singer/songwriter in her generated one of the most memorable songs of the 1960s:

> *I came upon a child of god*
> *He was walking along the road*
> *And i asked him, where are you going*
> *And this he told me*
> *I'm going on down to yasgur's farm*
> *I'm going to join in a rock 'n' roll band*
> *I'm going to camp out on the land*
> *I'm going to try an' get my soul free*
> *We are stardust*
> *We are golden*
> *And we've got to get ourselves*
> *Back to the garden*

Crosby, Stills, and Nash famously recorded the Woodstock anthem. However, the most memorable performance was Mitchell's elegant acoustic version at the Isle of Wight Festival in July 1970 in front of more than half a million fans.

By the end of the decade, she described the house as too comfortable and holding too many memories. She left the Canyon in 1970 for a house she built on the British Columbia coast in Canada. In 1971 she released the "Blue" album. Mitchell wrote it in the wake of her break-up with Graham Nash as reflected in songs like "My Old Man" and "River". The autobiographical reality of the songs and Mitchell's soprano voice garnered widespread praise for the album. The song "California" was written in France and reflects her affection for the state:

> *Oh California I'm coming home*
> *Oh make me feel good rock 'n' roll band*
> *I'm your biggest fan*
> *California I'm coming...*

Mama Cass Elliot

If Joni Mitchell was the hippie goddess of Laurel Canyon, then Mama Cass Elliot was the Canyon's earth mother. Her powerful voice drew in fans when she performed in Greenwich Village clubs in New York and Georgetown clubs in Washington. Her personality filled the stage, often leaving her bandmates in the shadows. After several unsuccessful groups, Denny Doherty introduced her to John and Michelle Philips in their NYC apartment. They dropped acid together—the start of what would become a musical partnership.

[Mama Cass Elliot's First House in the Canyon]

When the LA folk-rock explosion and the British invasion upturned the NYC music world, Elliot found herself without a band and moved to LA in 1965. Soon after, there was a knock on her door, John and Michele Philips along with Doherty had just arrived from their cross-country trek to LA. Shortly thereafter, the *Mamas and Pappas* were born.

When the group started gaining some success, Elliot found a house in Laurel Canyon (2044 Stanley Hills, Dr.). She reunited with David Crosby, her drug pal from NYC folk days. Very quickly she became the queen of the canyon; she knew everyone, and they knew her. She was a fixture at the Whiskey and the Troubadour.

She created relationships and brought people together as friends, lovers, or bandmates. She was the bridge that connected Crosby and Stills to the new Canadian in town, Graham Nash.

As the musical and financial success of the *Mamas and Pappas* grew, Elliot moved to Natalie Wood's former house at the top of the Canyon with a pool and a panoramic view (7708 Woodrow Wilson Dr.). This became a notorious party house for the Canyon, rivaling Micky Dolenz's. If she met a new singer in Hollywood she'd invite him to join her "salon" where humor, singing, and drugs were always in generous supply. Friends were always welcome, as long as they called first. As Elliot told *Rolling Stone* magazine:

> My house is a very free house. It's not a crash pad and people don't come without calling. But on an afternoon, especially on weekends, I always get a lot of delicatessen food in because I know David [Crosby] is going to come over for a swim and things are going to happen."

Graham Nash described Elliot in glowing terms: "she was *brilliant* and she *loved* friends and she loved to get high with all of us. She was the queen".

Cass House on Woodrow Wilson

Just as fast as the *Mamas and Papas* rise was their fall. They released three top-five studio albums in 1966-1967. Her lead vocals powered some of the best songs: "Words of Love", "Dancing in the Streets", and "I Call Your Name." Then internal musical and marital infidelities started their decline. Their 1968 album was their last successful release and then they disbanded.

Elliot embarked on a solo career with a modestly successful single/album in 1968, "Dream a Little Dream of Me". Her powerful voice was still there, but she was increasingly plagued by her drug use.

> *Stars shinin' bright above you*
> *Night breezes seem to whisper, "I love you"*
> *Birds singin' in the sycamore tree*
> *Dream a little dream of me*

Her failed live solo debut headlining at Caesars Palace in Las Vegas in 1968 was attributed to heroin use. Elliot continued to perform and was a very visible part of the LA music and television community. She was a frequent guest on TV variety shows from *The Smothers Brothers* to the *Mike Douglas Show*.

In July 1974, she performed a series of concerts at the London Palladium. When the last concert was over, she returned to her flat at the Curzon and died in her sleep at age 32 from a heart attack. Coincidentally, Elliot's good friend, Keith Moon of the *Who,* would die in the same room four years later. Her dream was over.

Linda Ronstadt

During Spring Break in 1965, a young University of Arizona student and amateur singer visited her friends in Southern California. During the visit, she went to the Trip, a club on the Sunset Strip where a hot new folk-rock band, *The Byrds,* was playing. Then and there, she started making plans to move to LA. At the end of the academic year, she told her parents. After a bit of family discussion, her father pulled out her grandfather's 1898 Martin guitar and told her "Now that you own a guitar, you will never be hungry." Linda Ronstadt headed off to Hollywood.

Ronstadt became part of the music scene at the Troubadour and the Ash Grove. She watched performances while practicing her craft at home in Santa Monica with two friends, and then they played at the Troubadour's Monday Hoot Night. Their band, *The Stone Ponies,* signed with Capitol Records in 1966 and their first two albums were released with modest success. Their successful third album featured her breakout single "Different Drums". By 1968 they were on tour as the opening act for *The Doors*. When the tour ended, the *Ponies* disbanded, and Ronstadt returned to LA to turn solo.

In 1968, she was briefly a tenant in Doug Dillard's home in the Canyon. Then she took up residence in Topanga Canyon, which was a sort of Laurel Canyon West—more rural, more eccentric, and filled with musicians. She released her first solo studio album in 1969, "Home Grown . . . And On My Mind" which charted her new course as a country-rock artist. As an acknowledgment of her Laurel/Topanga heritage, the back cover of the album was filmed at the same old stone house in Topanga as *The Notorious Byrd Brothers* album.

In 1970 she moved back to LA with JD Souther at the Highland-Camrose Bungalows (6809 Camrose Dr., Hollywood). Jackson Browne lived in the next bungalow. The Troubadour continued to be her home away from home as she developed her solo career.

At one Troubadour Hoot Night, she looked for backup musicians. She was impressed by a new group from Texas and invited them to tour with her. Then they collected a few more backup musicians. One day when practicing at her Hollywood bungalow, their voices merged into a rich harmony. This is the day *The Eagles* began to fly. They went on tour with her and played on her third album, "Linda Ronstadt".

[The Camrose bungalows. The *Eagles* band members and Jackson Browne also lived here in other bungalows.]

Her fifth solo album, "Heart Like a Wheel", established her reputation and rose to #1 on the Billboard chart. The album's top single, "You're No Good," also reached #1. This cemented her position as the independent "First Lady of Rock".

Feelin' better now that we're through
Feelin' better, 'cause I'm over you
I learned my lesson, it left a scar
Now I see how you really are

You're no good, You're no good, You're no good
Baby, you're no good

She knew everyone at the Troubadour and in Laurel Canyon, and they knew her. She sang with them and in their homes, but never lived in the Canyon culture. They all were impressed by her doe-eye look and powerful voice—and her independence. She has also said that she didn't fully fit into the culture of the Canyon. She was a woman rather than a hedonist. She didn't do drugs and that was central to Canyon life. She is quoted as saying: "I . . . didn't want to embrace the values that have been so completely embraced by that city [Los Angeles]. Are you glamorous? Are you rich? Are you important? Do you have clout? It's just not me and it never was me." What they did share was a love of music. She moved to San Francisco in 1987.

The richness and diversity of her solo-artist career are impressive. She released 24 studio albums, earned 10 Grammy awards, won the Grammy Lifetime Achievement Award, and was inducted into the Rock and Roll Hall of Fame. The titles of the top five on her playlist evoke memories of her distinctive voice: "When Will I Be Loved", "Love Is Like a Heatwave", "You're No Good", "It's So Easy", and "Blue Bayou". Ronstadt, Dolly Parton, and Emmylou Harris share a star on the Hollywood Walk of Fame. To expand musically, she sang Gilbert and Sullivan's "The Pirates of Penzance" on Broadway, earning a Tony nomination. Toward the end of the 1980s, she returned to her Mexican-American roots with an album of traditional Mexican folk songs., and her career continued for several more decades. Few female single artists in America could match her career, more than proving her grandfather was correct.

Judy Collins

Judy Collins' special relationship with artists in Laurel Canyon showed the mystical power of this community. Collins was based in New York and saw this as her comfortable home. But in 1967 she was introduced to Joni Mitchell over the phone, and heard her sing "Both Sides Now". This song became a hugely successful single for Collins and Mitchell's first big success as a writer. When Collins visited LA to record or give a concert, she would often visit Mitchell's home in the Canyon where they would talk and sing together.

In June 1968, Collins returned to LA to record a new album at the Electra Studios. At a production party, she met Stephen Stills. His role in her life is captured by the first sentence in her autobiography "Nineteen Sixty-Eight, the year I met and fell in love with Stephen Stills". Stills played backup on her album "Who Knows Where the Time Goes." At the end of the day Stills stayed late at Electra, and recorded an "End of Recording" tape.

They began a deep yet turbulent bicoastal relationship. Stills would see Collins when he was in NYC, and she spent time with him when she was on tour or recording in LA. They even hired a real estate agent to show them houses, and debated whether to live in Laurel Canyon or Malibu.

They struggled with a long distant relationship: Stills in LA and Judy Collins in New York. The centrifugal forces of their lives pulled them in different directions and their relationship began to fray. During her visit for the 1969 Grammys, Stills brought her a vintage Martin 00-42 guitar as a gift and first sang "Suite: Judy Blue Eyes" to her as a plea for their relationship.

> *It's getting to the point where*
> *I'm no fun anymore*
> *I am sorry*
> *Sometimes it hurts so badly, I must cry out loud*
> *"I am lonely"*
> *I am yours, you are mine, you are what you are*
> *You make it hard*

After he finished, she said: "Oh, Stephen, it's such a beautiful song. But it's not winning me back." Lots of hearts were broken in Laurel Canyon.

They continued but now as friends. In 1972 he called her just to talk about life. That night it stimulated a dream, and the next day she wrote the words to "House". It was a reflection on their life together.

> *When the Winter finds you, you fly to where it's summer*
> *Rooms that face the ocean, moonlight on your bed*
> *Mermaids swift as dolphins paint the air with diamonds*
> *You are like a seagull as you said*

In 2007, someone sent Graham Nash the "End of Recording" tape that Stills had made in 1968, and he forwarded it to Stills. It contained the original acoustic versions of some of Stills's early songs including "Suite: Judy Blue Eyes" and "Judy". Stills sent a CD of the songs to Collins, who heard them for the first time. In her autobiography, she wrote that it was like receiving a valentine 40 days later. When Stills and Collins finally reunited after 50 years for a concert series in 2017, she still had the Martin guitar.

CALIFORNIA ROAD TRIPS: MUSIC 1960-1970s

***

These last two chapters give a sense of the closeness of the Laurel Canyon music community. They wrote together, sang together, lived together, and often loved together. The mystique of Laurel Canyon ended in the early 1970s, but the decline started sooner. Three things brought about the change. One was the inevitable shift in the public's music tastes. The hippie culture of Laurel Canyon's early years fit the Aquarian spirit of the times. But as artists reaped the rewards of their success, many moved to Benedict Canyon, Bel Air, or points west. Music styles and public preferences also don't last forever. Music rivals were already on the horizon. As David Crosby prophetically said in 1965: "Change is where it's at".

A second factor was the traumatic shocks at the end of the 1960s. A new hippie family had joined the Southern California music community, led by Charles Manson. After his prison release in 1967, Manson assembled a cult following built around a Doomsday culture and his music. Manson tried to sell his songs to music companies or the artists he met in SoCal. His response to rejection was to attack the music community. He sent his followers to kill all the occupants of the home of Terry Melcher, a record producer who had rejected his songs.

The Manson Family killings of Sharon Tate and the others renting Melcher's house and the LaBianca murders occurred in August 1969. The violence shook the Laurel Canyon community to its core. The Canyon residents personally knew the Manson Family. The Family had attended parties in Mama Cass's home. Manson knew Neil Young when they both lived in Topanga Canyon; Young and Dennis Wilson of the *Beach Boys* helped him connect to music executives. The Family lived for a while at Wilson's home, and camped at the Philips' home in Bel Air. The *Beach Boys* recorded one of Manson's songs. Polanski initially accused John Philips of the murders as retribution for his affair with Michele Philips. The links between the Canyon people and The Family were numerous.

Consequently, many people no longer viewed the hippie, alternative lifestyle as something wonderful or at least benign. People stopped picking up hitchhikers in the canyons. Hippie-types and groupies were now suspect because not everything was peace and happiness. Just as Woodstock in August 1969 showed the positivity of the alternative movement, the Altamont Speedway Free Festival a few months later showed a potential dark side.

Finally, the incursion of hard drugs eroded the culture of the Canyon. Pot and psychedelics had nurtured the Canyon's hippie culture and a sense of positive creativity. But hard drugs had a destructive force on the canyon community. Jimi Hendrix died of a barbiturate overdose in September 1970. In October 1970, Janis Joplin died of a heroin overdose at the nearby Landmark Motor Hotel in Hollywood (room 105). The capstone (or gravestone) was Jim Morrison's death in Paris in July 1971. David Crosby's long-time use of hard drugs led to convictions for heroin and cocaine possession and a stint in the Texas State Prison in 1985.

Being in Laurel Canyon in the 1960s was a thing to enjoy and celebrate. You could walk the streets and hear beautiful music wafting from a balcony, or enjoy the positive vibes of the community. Today there are still signs of the past, but the Canyon of the 1960s no longer exists.

5. THE BEATLES IN LA

The Beatles are arguably the best-known band of the 1960s (or beyond). They are admittedly a British band, yet they had a continuing long relationship with Los Angeles and the music community in LA. Their impact on music was exceptional—twelve studio albums in the US, most of which reached a #1 ranking--and 22 singles that did equally well on the Billboard chart. In early 1964 they accounted for nearly half of the single record sales in the United States.

The criteria for including *The Beatle*s is more than just record sales. Although they were not from LA or based in LA during their productive years, they were closely linked to the LA music community. Capitol Records in Hollywood was their American record publisher in the early 1960s. This generated extensive business ties, especially since Capitol would restructure the UK albums for the American market. When "I Want to Hold Your Hand" was released in December 1963, it resonated throughout Southern California. This began a two-way interaction between the *Beatles* and California artists. For example, the *Beatles* followed the work of the *Beach Boys* in the early 1960s and this became an ongoing interchange. The Laurel Canyon folk-rock community was also strongly influenced by the early Beatles' records.

The *Beatles* also were culturally part of the 1960s LA music scene separate from their British roots. Although not residents of Laurel Canyon, they were early adopters of the sex, drugs, and rock-and-roll mantra. When they visited LA on tour or outside of tours they met and mingled with the community as described here. In later years, John, Paul, George, and Ringo lived in SoCal for extended periods. They registered major experiences here and left their mark on LA. So this deserves their inclusion as part of LA's musical history with some illustrative examples.

The 1964 Beatles Tour

The *Beatles*' first LA concert was funded by Bob Eubanks, a 26-year-old radio DJ and proprietor of several nightclubs. Because of his radio experience, he knew the band would be popular. Traditional promoters were skeptical. So Eubanks mortgaged his house to underwrite the LA concert. How prescient. The *Beatles*' blockbuster movie, "Hard Day's Night", came out on August 11th in the US.

The *Beatles* arrived at LAX as part of their first US tour on August 18, 1964. After the LA Biltmore hotel canceled their reservations because of the mass of fans, actor Reginald Owen offered his Bel Air house for rent (356 Saint Pierre Road). It was there that Lennon jumped into the pool fully clothed, and the foursome played cowboys and Indians with toy pistols — a gift from Elvis Presley. Screaming girls surrounded the mansion crying out for their favorite Beatle.

[1964 Beatles Tour Stay]

The concert tickets at the Hollywood Bowl sold out quickly and the benches were full of screaming fans. The Beatles played a full setlist of their most popular songs. The trouble was that thousands of screaming fans made it almost impossible to hear. Capitol Records had sent a crew to record the concert for a live album. Instead, the screaming dominated the tapes.

The band rested two days in LA before the next stop on the tour. On one day, the Capitol Records exec who signed the *Beatles* threw a charity fundraiser in Brentwood. The *Beatles* were awed to meet Hollywood royalty: Edward G Robinson, Jack Benny, Vince Edwards, Jane Fonda, Rock Hudson, Dean Martin, James Stewart, and Groucho Marx. The next day they went to Burt Lancaster's house to watch the new Peter Sellers' film and then to Whisky a Go Go in the evening with Jayne Mansfield. This was their introduction to life in Los Angeles.

These four Liverpool lads left LA impressed by the fans, the music, and the city. Afterward, John Lennon commented: "The Hollywood Bowl was marvelous. It was the one we all enjoyed most, I think, even though it wasn't the largest crowd – because it seemed so important, and everybody was saying things. We got on, and it was a big stage, and it was great."

The 1965 Beatles Tour

By 1965 the *Beatles* dominated the popular music scene with their amazing list of hits. The band had also become more creative musically, going beyond the simple lyrics and heavy style of their first singles, and their hair grew longer. A month after their single "Help" was released, they came to Los Angeles as part of their second US tour.

The band rented Zsa Zsa Gabor's house (2850 Benedict Canyon Drive, Beverly Hills). Quickly the word spread, and fans stood across the gated entrance. This is where John, George, and Ringo took LSD, Roger McGuinn of the *Byrds* played Ravi Shankar records, and Peter Fonda (also on acid) kept telling John "I know what it's like to be dead." John wrote "She Said, She Said" about their experience. The house has been in reconstruction for several years, and mostly has workers' trucks in the driveway, but is visible from below along the Benedict Canyon.

On August 27th they fulfilled a long-time wish to meet Elvis Presley at his rented house in Bel Air (565 Perugia Way, Los Angeles). It was awkward at first as the *Beatles* were in awe of Elvis and mostly stared at "The King". Eventually, they broke out the guitars and had a small jam session. George Harrison later said it was one of the highlights of the 1965 tour.

[Zsa Zsa's Benedict Cyn. house before recent renovation]

On August 29th and 30th they performed to sellout crowds at the Hollywood Bowl. They played a full set of their songs, but who could tell? According to a Hollywood Bowl usher:

"It was pandemonium. 18,000 fans were screaming at the top of their lungs. Those who couldn't get tickets gate crashed from the hills above the Bowl and came rolling down the hills and through the bushes. And you couldn't hear the *Beatles* play because of the screaming fans."

Capitol Records recorded both nights and excerpted the best of the audio. They later issued the album "Live at the Hollywood Bowl". The original album release has become a valuable collector's item among Beatles fans in LA.

The 1966 Beatles Tour

Los Angeles was the next to last stop on the band's 1966 tour to promote the newly released "Revolver" album. The album's tracks were technically sophisticated and marked the start of the group's psychedelic period, reflecting an intermixing of Eastern philosophy and music, counter-culture themes, and their drug trip experiences. It topped the US charts for six weeks. "Here, There and Everywhere" was one of McCartney's finest songs, inspired by the *Beach Boys'* track "God Only Knows".

This was a contentious tour because John Lennon's statement—that the *Beatles* were more popular than Jesus—stimulated a conservative backlash at early tour stops in several cities. Other journalists asked them to explain the lyrics of songs such as "Yellow Submarine" and "Good Day Sunshine" All innocent lyrics according to the band.

They arrived in LA on August 24 and stayed at a rented home in the Hollywood Hills at the end of a winding road (7655 Curson Terrace). The original house has been recently replaced by a 10+ million-dollar mansion. But the magnificent view of LA is still the same.

The guys had a day of rest and spent it meeting with the *Byrds* and the *Mamas and The Papas*. In the evening, Capitol Records threw a party where Hollywood movie stars celebrated the *Beatles'* success.

On the next day, Brian and Carl Wilson of the Beach Boys visited. The *Beach Boys* work set a standard for the *Beatles* when they were starting their rise to fame three years earlier. The dramatic evolution of the *Beatles'* music stimulated Brian Wilson to write "Pet Sounds", and so it went. They made each other better songwriters and musicians.

The concert was on August 28th. The previous concerts at the Hollywood Bowl could only accommodate 18,000 and so the 1966 concert was held at Dodger Stadium which seats 40,000. The band faced major security problems to get to the concert because of the venue's layout and the mass of fans. An armored car drove them to the stadium. After a successful concert comprised of their standard setlist of 11 songs, the band tried to leave, at first unsuccessfully as the crowd proved too much even for an armored car.

This was their penultimate live concert. After their final show in San Francisco, they stopped touring. The wear and tear on the band and the time commitment were too large. Thereafter the *Beatles* became a studio band, recording new songs in their UK studio. They continue to visit LA individually to perform, but never again as the *Beatles*. Paul McCartney's last solo concert in Los Angeles in 2019 was at Dodger Stadium with Ringo Starr joining him for "Sgt. Pepper's Lonely Hearts Club Band" and "Helter Skelter". A magical night, more than half a century after the 1966 concert.

Harrison in Hollywood

Another notable event in the *Beatles'* ties to LA came during a George Harrison visit in 1967. He had a direct flight from London to LAX and immediately went to a rented house on a winding road above the Sunset Strip (1567 Blue Jay Way). He was waiting for the Beatles publicist to arrive for a meeting. It was getting foggy, it was getting late, and he was getting tired.

George sat down on the Hammond organ in the living room and started to play around. Gradually the lyrics and music began to blend. The publicist's delay led to "Blue Jay Way" which appeared on the "Magical Mystery Tour".

There's a fog upon L.A.
And my friends have lost their way
We'll be over soon they said
Now they've lost themselves instead

Please don't be long
Please don't you be very long
Please don't be long
Or I may be asleep

It was George's creative genius, or maybe the musical karma of the house. Two years later, Paul Simon stayed at the same rental house and wrote "Bridge over Troubled Waters" there.

Lennon's Lost Weekend

In the fall of 1973, John Lennon and Yoyo Ono were struggling with their relationship. Lennon explained that he and Yoko were taking a break from one another. Yoko simply kicked him out and sent him to Los Angeles with their assistant, May Ping, as consort. Lennon called it his "Lost Weekend", but the LA half of the weekend lasted seven months.

[John Lennon's LC Hideaway]

They flew into LAX on September 19th and moved into Lou Adler's house in Bel Air because Adler was away (after a while they moved to the Beverly Wilshire Hotel). Lennon and May Ping also often used Elliot Mintz's house in Laurel Canyon (8522 Oak Ct.). It was a place where they could feel safe from prying eyes.

Lennon had plenty to keep him busy, Capitol Records was doing the final preparations for the release of his "Mind Games" album. LA was also convenient because he knew lots of people there, and Ringo was a frequent LA visitor. John and Phil Spector started work on a new album at A&M records. He reunited with his son Julian Lennon for the first time in four years. They enjoyed the time together, especially the multiple trips to Disneyland. John visited old and new friends in LA. In the meantime, he began drinking and enjoying the pleasures of his lost weekend—all the while phoning Yoko in the hope he could come home to New York City.

Then Lennon/Pang moved to the beach. Lennon rented the house originally built by Louis B. Mayer of MGM, and later owned by Peter Lawford, John F. Kennedy's brother-in-law (625 Palisades Beach Rd., Santa Monica). Some claim that Lawford arranged a tryst between one or more of the Kennedys and Marilyn Monroe at the house. Lennon and May Ping used that bedroom.

When the album with Spector stalled, Lennon started a new album project "Pussycats" with

[Lawford House on Palisades Beach Rd.]

Harry Nilsson. This kept him busy, as well as visits from his old friends. Ringo visited the beach house, and eventually Paul McCartney who was in Hollywood to produce a record. John and Paul took up guitars and played some of their old favorites. The last photo of John and Paul together was taken at the beach house. The last Lennon/Ping residence in LA was in the Hollywood Hills (8818 Thrasher Ave.).

Despite his emotional distractions and drinking binges in LA, this was a productive period. Capitol Records released "Mind Games" in October. The Pussycats" album started in Los Angeles was released in 1974.

In mid-April 1974, Lennon and Ping boarded a flight from LA to New York. The "lost weekend" wasn't over, it would continue for seven more months in NYC. But Lennon returned more rejuvenated and ready to write and sing.

George's Last Visit

In the fall of 2001, Paul McCartney was renting a beautiful estate in Beverly Hills (9536 Heather Rd.), which he later purchased. Ringo also owned a home in Beverly Hills, as well as Laguna Beach. George Harrison was receiving treatment at the Oncology Institute of Southern Switzerland after undergoing lung cancer surgery earlier in the year. Simultaneously he was writing music to record with his son, Dhani. Ringo visited him there to say goodbye. When the Swiss experts gave him a negative prognosis, he boarded a plane to the United States and another expert in New York. Then on to Los Angeles on a private jet and a consultation at the UCLA Medical Center.

George spent his final days in Paul's house. Ravi Shankar was there playing for him as his last days passed. He died there on November 29, 2001. He was cremated at the Hollywood Forever Cemetery in Hollywood, and his ashes were later scattered at Allahabad in India, where the Ganges, Yamuna, and Saraswati rivers converge. When news of George's death spread among his fans, his signature song "My Sweet Lord" rose to #1 on the UK charts.

[McCartney house on Heather Rd., Beverly Hills]

Hollywood Walk of Fame

In a different sense, the *Beatles* will never leave LA. Hollywood's tribute to the *Beatles* is marked by stars along the famous Walk of Fame. John Lennon was the first Beatle to receive his own star posthumously on Sept. 30, 1988. The *Beatles* band received a joint star on Christmas Day, 1998. Their star is at the west entrance to the Walk of Fame, next to Elvis Presley's star and the "Four Silver Ladies" statue at the corner of Hollywood Blvd. and La Brea Avenue (7080 Hollywood Blvd. on the traffic island).

[7080 Hollywood Blvd/La Brea on the traffic island]

Harrison posthumously received his star on April 14, 2009; Paul McCartney and Tom Hanks spoke at the induction.

Ringo's ceremony was on February 8, 2010; Joe Walsh from *Ringo's All-Star Band* and *The Eagles* spoke at the event. Finally, Neil Young spoke at McCartney's ceremony on February 9, 2012. All four of the stars for John, Paul, George, and Ringo are located next to each other at 1750 N. Vine Street. So if you want to see all the *Beatles*, take a walk to the front entrance of the Capitol Records building.

50 Years Later

Los Angeles' most recent celebration of the *Beatles* came at the 50th anniversary of their 1964 tour stop in LA. The Hollywood Bowl hosted a concert of contemporary artists performing the *Beatles*' 1964 playlist, from "I Want to Hold Your Hand," to "A Hard Day's Night". After the intermission, they featured classics such as "Strawberry Fields," "Hey Jude," and "All You Need is Love". Bob Eubanks, who organized the 1964 concert, was there to represent the link to the past. He welcomed fans to the Bowl, shook hands, shared stories, and took selfies. It was a special night for the many fans who were there at the *Beatles'* original concerts, especially the usher from 1965.

6. POP STARS

In the midst of the folk-rock era of the 1960s, another music genre emerged. Instead of the heavy rock sound of the Canyon, the music was light and upbeat. Instead of the introspective writing of Laurel Canyon artists, often tinged with counter-culture imagery, these musicians had fun and uplifting lyrics. Instead of social commentary, the lyrics were often secondary to a danceable beat. While folk-rock lyrics might make you think about society or politics, this new genre made you smile. These bands were described as "bubble gum rock", "champagne soul", or "soft rock". In most instances, it was "sex, drugs, and rock" without the sex and drugs.

Some of these artists were native or semi-native Californians. Others were drawn to Los Angeles by the shift of record production to the West Coast. Hollywood's Capitol Records became a major actor because of the *Beatles*, and up-and-coming groups recorded in their famous studios. Phil Specter perfected his hit-making "Wall of Sound" at the Gold Star Studio (6252 Santa Monica Blvd., LA). Brian Wilson of *The Beach Boys*' often preferred the sound from Studio 3 at Western Recorders (6050 Sunset Blvd., LA), even though the band recorded at other studios for their effects, and their music was on the Capitol label. Sunset Sound (6650 Sunset Blvd., LA) had a split personality, recording music for Walt Disney by day and *The Doors* at night. The list of artists using Sunset Sound's three main studios reads like a Who's Who of rock music (with a bit of Disney in the mix). In the 1970s, the Sound Factory (6357 Selma Ave.) became one of the busiest studios in Hollywood. And soon a new group of artists would fill these studios.

Sonny and Cher

One singer in this book probably holds the record for her early appearance in Laurel Canyon. The first line in Cher's autobiography (*The First Time*) reads "My first memory. I was four years old and living in Laurel Canyon." In 1963 Cher dropped out of high school to pursue a music career. Sonny Bono was a struggling songwriter who worked for Phil Spector. Their first time together was on a double date, and they disagree on who was with whom on that night. Sonny soon after "coincidentally" moved into the same apartment building where Cher lived (7214 Fountain Ave., Los Angeles). When Cher lost her job at See's Candies, she moved in with Sonny in a strictly platonic relationship.

Sonny was more than a decade older and more experienced in life and the record business. He thought of himself as Cher's mentor. His goal was to turn Cher into a star. He brought her to Specter's recording studio where she started to perform as a background singer. Her first record was "I Love You Ringo", a novelty song under a pseudonym. They were struggling artists, who moved into a Laurel Canyon house with their manager to save money. One night, Sonny woke Cher with a new song he had written for them, "I Got You, Babe". It was their first single that rose to #1 on the chart and captured the nature of their relationship.

They say we're young and we don't know
We won't find out until we grow
Well I don't know if all that's true
Cause you got me, and baby I got you

Sonny & Cher were launched. Their first album "Look at Us" was released in August 1965. It rose to #2 on Billboard. Their publicity machine had *Sonny & Cher* off to a running start. They toured the UK as the *Beatles* were touring the US, they appeared on the Ed Sullivan Show and Hullabaloo. Sonny stood out because of his long hair and bobcat fur vest; Cher nurtured her hippie look with long hair and bellbottoms. One critic said they were like two misfits, who together matched each other's needs.

Their second album appeared in 1967 and rose to #34 on the charts. With their newfound success, they moved from Encino (1651 Academia Dr.) and bought a mansion in Bel Air (364 St. Cloud Rd.), surrounded by the affluent and established. Yet even delivery people saw the old Sonny, who loved to chat and tipped well.

They were pop music's #1 couple, except that they weren't married (they privately corrected this). Their third album in 1967 garnered fewer sales and less positive reviews. Cher's solo album sales were also declining. They were on a downward spiral and struggled to find a new approach. As Cher later said: "hippies thought we were square, and squares thought we were hippies."

[Sonny and Cher Bel Air Mansion. In 1968 there was no gate]

By 1969, they released 3 *Sonny & Cher* albums, 6 Cher solo albums, and 2 low-budget movies that Sonny produced. The duo started touring on the nightclub circuit and drawing on their past success. They developed a new routine mixing their music and humor. The head of CBS programming saw one of their shows and offered them a TV contract.

In 1971, the "Sonny & Cher Comedy Hour" started taping. Although still unconventional, gone was Sonny's bobcat vest as well as Cher's bellbottoms and counter-culture clothes. Instead, they hosted a variety show appealing to a broader audience. The show was a top 20 hit and ran for four seasons. They sang, performed skits, and welcomed new guests each week. It was an adventure to visit the set at the famous CBS Television City (7800 Beverly Blvd.)

The workload of the TV show and their continued touring was a heavy burden and Sonny's desire to organize their lives pushed their relationship to the brink. In November 1972 Cher told Sonny she was leaving. They continued to co-star on the TV show until its last episode in May 1974. In July 1975 their divorce was final.

Cher moved on to a spectacularly successful career as a movie star (20 movies) and singer (26 studio albums). She had a #1 single on the Billboard chart in six consecutive decades. On April 11, 1988, Cher won the best actress Oscar for "Moonstruck". The next day, Sonny was elected mayor of Palm Springs. In 1994, he was elected to the U.S. House of Representatives. He was the only member of Congress with a #1 pop single. Their relationship continued until Sonny died in 1998, and Cher gave his eulogy.

The Fifth Dimension

Another Los Angeles group formed about the same time in the 1960s, but with a very different sound and a very different look. Lamonte McLemore was putting together a singing group and started with his UCLA girlfriend, Marilyn McCoo. They filled out the quintet with Florence LaRue, Billy Davis, and Ron Townson. They became the *Fifth Dimension.*

They described their music as "champagne soul". In 1965 they covered the *Mamas and Papas'* "Go Where You Wanna Go" and added a little soul. It outsold the *M&P*'s version. Their 1967 breakthrough single was "Up – Up and Way". The song hit #7 on the charts and won five Grammy Awards. As a black soul group distinct from the Motown sound, they gained a nationwide audience.

Their album of the same title also broke into the top 10. Between 1967 and 1971 they released 6 albums, and 5 rose to the top 25 on Billboard. Songs by Laura Nyro, "Stoned Soul Picnic" and "Wedding Bell Blues", reached the top 10 with the *Fifth Dimension*'s special harmonies and soul-full music. Their cover of the theme song from the musical *Hair*, "Aquarius/Let the Sunshine in" became synonymous with the feeling of the 1960s. It also topped the pop charts for six straight weeks. It won a Grammy for Record of the Year and another for Best Pop Vocal Performance by a Group.

In the mid-1970s the group's popularity seemed to flatten out and record sales followed. McCoo and Davis had married in 1969 and wanted to start their solo careers. Finally, in 1975 McCoo and Davis left the group, which continued with Florence LaRue in the lead.

When the moon is in the Seventh House
And Jupiter aligns with Mars
Then peace will guide the planets
And love will steer the stars
This is the dawning of the Age of Aquarius

In 1977, they lived in Encino, neighbors to Sonny and Cher and other celebrities. One night they found a burning cross on their lawn, which was attributed to the KKK. They moved to Beverly Hills as their success expanded. McCoo/Davis then embarked on their own successful duo career and later moved to their current home on a gated private street (9911 Mark Pl., BH).

They were path-breaking artists in an era of racial tension, with music that transcended racial lines. 50 years later they are still married, recording, touring, and letting the sunshine in.

Loving Spoonful and John Sebastian

When the *Mugwamps* disbanded in 1965, two groups were formed. Cass Elliot and Denny Doherty became half of the *Mamas and Papas*, while John Sebastian and Zal Yanovsky went about forming the *Lovin' Spoonful*.

Although the band and its studio were in New York, Sebastian also took up part-time residence in Laurel Canyon. Some stories claim that *Crosby, Stills, and Nash's* first harmonies were actually in Sebastian's house and not Joni Mitchell's. But who remembers facts from the 1960s?

Sebastian was a singer-songwriter and his song, "Do You Believe in Magic", was their first single released in July 1965. The lyrics weren't quite like the *Doors*':

Do you believe in magic in a young girl's heart
How the music can free her whenever it starts?
And it's magic if the music is groovy
It makes you feel happy like an old-time movie
I'll tell you about the magic, and it'll free your soul
But it's like trying to tell a stranger 'bout-a rock and roll

Then came a series of other top ten singles in 1965-66: "You Didn't Have to Be So Nice", "Daydream", "Did You Ever Have to Make Up Your Mind?", and "Summer in the City". The band quickly developed a national following for its upbeat style. Band members described their performances as "good-time music". The producers for the *Monkees* TV show also considered the Spoonful for the show, before casting their own band.

Then the bond holding the band together started the fray. One member left, and another was forced out. Finally, John Sebastian left the band in 1968 to pursue a solo career. He initially worked on the music for a Broadway play. He moved to LA after his divorce in 1969 and moved into a commune in the Hollywood Hills. The Farm was a 46-acre artistic community (where an apartment complex now stands at 3600 Barham Blvd.). Mama Cass and Linda Ronstadt were frequent visitors to The Farm. Tie-Dye Annie taught Sebastian how to tie-dye and this became his obsessive hobby. Then he bought a white Levi jacket to dye:

> "I wasn't going to rush it or just toss it in the dye, I'm going to tie little teeny parts and let it just take forever and that's what I did with the Woodstock jacket, just one part at a time. So there are a lot of colors on that jacket and they sort of represent The Farm because I would dip into other people's pots whenever possible."

Later that summer he went to the Woodstock concert to hear his friends play. When the concert was delayed because of the rain and water causing an electrical risk, the organizers looked for an acoustic fill-in. Sebastian was on stage. He performed a mix of his new songs and two from the *Lovin' Spoonful* days and became a part of Woodstock history—wearing his tie-dyed Levis jacket.

Sebastian had modest success as a solo artist until 1975 when his song "Welcome Back" became the theme song of the television sitcom "Welcome Back, Kotter". The single rose to #1 on the Billboard chart. Today he lives in a modest ranch house in the San Fernando Valley and continues to tour.

***

Music plays many roles in life. One is to make people happy. These pop groups and many others like *The Association* and *America* gave people respite from the social and political commentary of the day. And making people smile is a good legacy.

7. THE SECOND GENERATION

Toward the end of the 1960s, many of the artists who put Laurel Canyon on the map had moved on. John and Michele Philips moved to a mansion in Beverly Hills to the consternation of their neighbors. David Crosby had moved west to Beverly Glen. Jim Morrison began his vagabond life in hotels and rentals. In 1970, Joni Mitchell moved back to Canada. Stephen Stills moved on to Malibu. Neil Young moved to Topanga Canyon.

By the late 1960s, the music scene in Los Angeles was also undergoing a major transformation. Record producers such as David Geffen and Lou Adler recruited new artists to fill their rosters. The number of recording studios and studio musicians multiplied across the Southland. Capitol Records' success with the Beatles attracted other up-and-coming musicians. And the mystique of Laurel Canyon, even if fading, drew them in in the hills.

This began what some call "the second generation" of Laurel Canyon music artists. Some represented the maturation of young artists who moved from supporting roles to construct their own bands or solo careers. Some came from Southern California and were too young to be active during the early 1960s. Others came from New York or other parts of the United States, drawn by LA's new reputation as the center of the American music network. Many of these new artists took up residence in Laurel Canyon, at least temporarily. They injected new creative energy into the music community running into the 1970s (and beyond) before moving on themselves.

The Eagles

The *Eagles* formed in Los Angeles in 1971 although none of the founding members was originally from California. Don Henley was a talented drummer and singer from Linden, TX. He grew up surrounded by blues music and started as a drummer in a Dixieland jazz band. He often recalls the appearance of the *Beatles*' music on the scene as a "bolt of lightning". Meanwhile, in Detroit, Michigan (Motown's home) a young, long-haired singer and songwriter named Glenn Frey was about to attend the Fab Four's gig at the Olympia Stadium. Henley and Frey didn't yet perceive how this inspiration would eventually drive them to sell even more albums than the Beatles.

Glenn Frey's career in Michigan took off after Bob Seger started to "mentor" him, and California was the obvious next stop. On his very first day in LA, Frey met two people. One was the first celebrity he ever saw with his own eyes: David Crosby. The second was JD Souther. Together, they went to Sunset Blvd. and made friends with Jackson Browne. A propitious first 24 hours.

Soon afterward, Henley and Souther ended up sharing a house in Echo Park (1020 Laguna Ave., Echo Park). They had the top floor and Browne was in a tiny basement studio. Browne taught Frey how to write songs, and sometimes he reciprocated (see Browne section below).

One can easily see the lasting imprint of Browne's songwriting method ("thought, persistence") on Frey's and the *Eagles*' musical perfectionism.

Frey, Souther, and Browne were regulars at the Troubadour. This is where Frey first met Henley – who moved to LA to play drums for Kenny Rogers. Linda Ronstadt heard them play at the Troub and invited them to be part of her backup band on tour. The Frey/Henley harmonies were first performed in Linda Ronstadt's living room at the Camrose Bungalows in Hollywood (see Chapter 5).

It didn't take long before the huge ambitions of Frey and Henley led them to leave Ronstadt's band to form their own. She not only accepted their decision but also suggested that they take another of her musicians with them: multi-instrumentalist Bernie Leadon (formerly with the *Flying Burrito Brothers*). With the addition of Randy Meisner, a high-pitched singer and bass player, the *Eagles* were complete.

[Frey/Browne house on Laguna Ave.]

Now, they just needed to sign for a record label. David Geffen's Asylum Records was the most obvious match. Unlike the previous generation of Southern California musicians, the Eagles recorded the first half of their records in England. Geffen and the *Eagles* wanted to be produced by the top-notch rock engineer, Glynn Johns, who had already produced *Rolling Stones*, *The Who,* and *Led Zeppelin* among others. Unlike the previous generation, they accepted a record studio policy of "no drugs, no alcohol". Similar to the previous generation, however, they made wide use of both drugs and alcohol to fuel their creativity. Frey and Henley shared a house in Laurel Canyon at the corner of Ridpath and Kirkwood (8301 Ridpath Dr.). It was a notorious sex-drugs and oftentimes rock n' roll party house: the Kirkwood Casino and Health Club. They also hosted famous late-night card games after watching Monday night football. Even Joni Mitchell came over to play poker.

[Frey/Henley House on Ridpath Dr.]

The cover of their 1972 eponymous album, "Eagles" found inspiration in a night on peyote in the desert at the Joshua Tree National Monument. The album broke into the top 25 and produced three major hits: "Take It Easy", "Witchy Woman", and "Peaceful Easy Feeling".

The group started moving up with this success. Frey and Henley rented a fancy house in Coldwater Canyon in Beverly Hills (1740 La Fontaine Ct.). This is where they wrote the top 20 album, "On the Border". Later they would rent an even fancier house at the top of the Trousdale Estate where they wrote "Lyin' Eyes. (1375 N Doheny Dr., Beverly Hills).

[Frey/Henley House on La Fontaine Ct.]

However, the band suffered from a lack of a coherent musical direction. As a result, they invited guitarist Don Felder to join them.

The outcome was the 1975 album, "One of These Nights". It quickly rose to #1 on the charts, 4x platinum, and the best-selling album of their history so far. Featuring songs like "Lyin' Eyes" and "Take it to the Limit"; the title track. "Lyin' Eyes" won a Grammy for best pop song of the year.

The album positioned the *Eagles* to embark on their most ambitious musical project. The rest was done by another change in the band line-up. Leadon and Frey had growing tensions about the band's direction. This eventually led Leadon to pour a beer on Frey's head as a sort of goodbye. Joe Walsh, an already reputable guitar hero with a passion for alcohol and a gift for room trashing, was the new band member. Frey loved his rock'n'roll attitude, which he would happily show off on a nightly basis at the band's usual "Third Encore" after the shows.

The first song of the new line-up became their trademark hit: "Hotel California". The harmonious textures developed by Felder and Walsh marked a departure from the country-rock sound of the previous albums. It moved the band to write an entire album around the concept of myth-making California through the hotel itself:

> *Mirrors on the ceiling,*
> *The pink champagne on ice*
> *And she said "We are all just prisoners here, of our own device"*
> *And in the master's chambers,*
> *They gathered for the feast*
> *They stab it with their steely knives,*
> *But they just can't kill the beast*

The album spent 8 weeks at #1 on the Billboard chart and eventually won the Grammy for record of the year in 1978, and another Grammy for "New Kid in Town".

The huge worldwide tour that followed further strained the personal relationships among band members. Meisner's reluctance to sing "Take it to the Limit" in concert, due to his concerns about not hitting the high notes, led to disputes and eventually his departure from the band. He was replaced by the same musician who had succeeded him in *Poco*, Timothy B. Schmit. After a painful three-year struggle, the *Eagles* released their next album, "The Long Run" in 1979. The album also rose to #1 on the charts and featured numerous hit singles including their possibly most famous ballad, Schmidt's "I Can't Tell You Why".

The Eagles were consciously constructed to be a successful mega-touring band with a distinct sound. Most parts of the band were interchangeable; if one member left they were replaced and the music played on. Nevertheless, the growing tensions cumulated into the band's break-up. On July 31, 1980, in Long Beach, CA, the animosity between Felder and Frey boiled over before their show in support of California Senator Alan Cranston. Frey and Felder spent the entire show telling each other about the beating each planned to administer backstage. After the show, Felder destroyed his cheapest guitar, jumped in his limo, and took off. It was the last gig of the *Eagles* until their reunion in 1994, which Frey described as a 14-year hiatus.

With five #1 singles, six #1 albums, and six Grammys, the *Eagles* were among the most successful musical acts of the 1970s in the US and certainly one of the most representative of the Southern California rock scene of the era. The group was inducted into the Rock and Roll Hall of Fame in 1998.

Carole King

Carole King was a second-generation artist of a different sort. Her early career was primarily as a highly successful songwriter in New York City. After breaking up with her boyfriend, she moved to California for a new start in late 1967. She got a small two-bedroom house at 8857 Wonderland Ave. close to other musician friends in Laurel Canyon. King changed from a hip New York City songwriter into a hippie singer-songwriter in Laurel Canyon. In her words, "she found herself."

King briefly joined a band, *The City*, with new friends in LA and her former boyfriend from New York. The band had limited success and soon folded. She began performing at the Troubadour and other LA venues, and continued to perfect her new style. For parts of 1969 and 1970, she toured as the opening act for James Taylor. Joni Mitchell, Taylor's new girlfriend, occasionally joined them on tour.

In January of 1971, King entered the A&M Records studio to record her second studio album. King wrote the songs in "Tapestry" at her home on Wonderland. The iconic cover photo was taken at the house's front window.

The album dramatically launched her second career as both a songwriter <u>and</u> a singer. It received four Grammy Awards in 1972, including album of the year. The lead singles from the album, "It's Too Late" and "I Feel the Earth Move", spent five weeks at #1 on the Billboard chart. It became a standout of contemporary music in America, earning a 13 times platinum sales rating by 2021.

King married her on/off boyfriend and music partner, Charlie Larkie, in September 1970. After the success of "Tapestry," they moved to a much larger French Revival-style house, complete with turrets (8815 Appian Way) at the top of Laurel Canyon.

Building on the success of "Tapestry" King wrote a second album, "Music" that was released at the end of 1972. It quickly rose to #1 in the charts, and for a while shared a top 10 ranking with "Tapestry". "Sweet Seasons" from the album broke into the top 10 as a single. Since King wrote most of "Music" at her new home, the cover featured her playing a grand piano in the new living room.

[King House on Wonderland]

Her success led to promotional tours, but eventually divorced Larkie. A new singer, Rick Evers, entered her life and this changed her trajectory. He wanted to produce her next album, so King left Ode Records. Evers also co-wrote some of the songs for the new album. When the album, "Music" was released in July 1977, only King's reputation kept it from failing. *Rolling Stone* called it the worst album of 1977. Love is blind, or at least tone-deaf.

Following a new life course, King and Evers moved to Idaho to pursue a rural communal life. They were married, but a year later Evers died from a drug overdose. She continued to write exquisite songs. But it took decades for her creative works to be high on the charts again and for her to gain the deserved career recognition for the artistry of her Laurel Canyon years.

[King House on Appian Way]

Beginning with Tapestry", King released 6 albums with Ode Records and produced by the legendary Lou Adler. All six peaked with a top 10 Billboard ranking and three reached #1. King's lyrics and songs were covered by many of the most talented artists of the 1970s. She was inducted into the Rock and Roll Hall of Fame in 2021.

Jackson Browne

Jackson Browne was a youngster by the standards of 1960s Laurel Canyon. He grew up in Orange County, CA. As a novice musician, he went to the weekend surf music concerts at the Rendezvous Ballroom in Newport Beach. After high school graduation in 1966, he joined the *Nitty Gritty Dirt Band* for a while and played at local venues. Then he moved to Laurel Canyon to be near the action.

Browne initially crashed at Paul Rothchild's notorious party house at 8524 Ridpath Dr. Then he moved down the street to the basement laundry room of his agent's house, Billy James, at 8504 Ridpath Dr. Today, the house serves as the Chilean consulate in LA, and must get strange visitors because of the house's earlier music history.

[Jackson Browne on Ridpath Dr.]

After a sojourn in NYC, he returned to LA. Browne was ever-present at the Ashgrove or the Troubadour, meeting new friends and impressing the young women with his soulful sensuality. His initial success was writing songs for other artists. The *Nitty Gritty Dirt Band* recorded a couple of his songs, and Nico recorded Browne's "These Days." Everyone knew him and liked him. But try as he might, he couldn't get a record deal of his own. Record companies said he wasn't quite there yet, for several years.

When he looked for his own place, a couple of friends told him about a rental at their building in Echo Park; the rent was $35 a month. Browne moved into a very small studio apartment and started working on his songs (see *Eagles* section above). The musician neighbors upstairs complained that their morning would begin with the loud whistling of Browne's teapot, and then Browne's piano playing the same stanza over and over again until it was right, then the next stanza for 20 times, etc.

Browne was working on a song, but couldn't figure out the ending. The upstairs neighbor, Glenn Frey, helped him finish the lyrics, and "Take it Easy" was born. Frey's key lyric:

> *It's a girl, my lord,*
> *in a flatbed Ford,*
> *slowing down to take a look at me*

David Crosby encouraged Browne to send a demo tape to David Geffen the hyperactive ambitious talent scout for Atlantic Records. Prodded by his secretary's reaction to Browne's photo, Geffen listened to the demo and wanted to sign Browne. The record company was less enthusiastic, leading to Geffen creating Asylum Records with Browne and *The Eagles* as his first two clients.

Browne released his first album in 1972, "Jackson Browne". The single from the album, "Doctor, My Eyes", reached #8 on the charts. David Crosby and Graham Nash added their harmonies to the single. After years of trying, Browne finally achieved success with Geffen as a mentor.

His second album evoked the concept of family in many ways. The album included vocals with his LA music family: David Crosby, Glen Frye, Elton John, Don Henley, Joni Mitchell, and Bonnie Rait. The album cover photo was taken at the historic Browne family home his grandfather built, The Abbey San Encino, in Highland Park.

Browne was on the road to success, touring with artists like Joni Mitchell and Ronstadt; then becoming the headliner. He improved as an artist and nurtured his fan base.

Browne's career followed an unusual pattern for Laurel Canyon artists. The first half dozen albums he released received increasing praise from the critics, and increasing sales. His 1980 album, "Hold Out" reached #1 on the Billboard chart. The album's two singles "Boulevard" and "That Girl Can Sing" both rose to the top 25.

Browne's career was also remarkable because it was enduring. Many artists count their success in terms of months, or years if they are lucky. After his #1 album in 1980, Browne released eight more albums with the most recent in 2014 (he says another album is now in the works). All of these albums ranked in the top 50 according to Billboard.

James Taylor and Carly Simon

James Taylor had a difficult adolescence. When other kids were in high school he was struggling with mental illness. When other kids were in college, he was struggling with mental illness coupled with drug addiction as he played in clubs in Greenwich Village. For a break, he moved to England in 1967. The following year Taylor auditioned for Apple Records playing a song he had written: "Something in the Way She Moves". This got him a contract with Apple and yielded George Harrison's version of "Something".

He returned to the United States and in 1969 relocated to California where he had a new contract with Warner Bros. Records. He had a very successful six-week run at the Troubadour earlier in 1969.

He finished his first US album, "Sweet Baby James," in late 1969. His New York friend and recent LA resident, Carole King, played piano on some cuts. Taylor had written some of the songs on his album while at a mental institution. To catch the earthy image of his music, the album cover photos were taken at The Farm on Barnham Blvd. (where John Sebastian lived after moving to LA in 1969). The album was released in February 1970. It rose to #3 on the Billboard chart and was nominated for a Grammy as the best album of the year.

The struggles of his earlier battles with mental illness and a friend's recent death by overdose led to the powerful top song from the album, "Fire and Rain":

Won't you look down upon me, Jesus?
You've got to help me make a stand
You've just got to see me through another day
My body's aching and my time is at hand
And I won't make it any other way

Oh, I've seen fire and I've seen rain
I've seen sunny days that I thought would never end
I've seen lonely times when I could not find a friend
But I always thought that I'd see you again

He initially crashed at the home of his agent, his producer, or any friend who would take him in. But very quickly he became part of the Laurel Canyon community and a regular at the Troubadour. Taylor went on tour to promote the new album and began a relationship with Joni Mitchell in July 1970. They toured together, wrote music together, and Taylor moved into her famous house on Lookout Mountain (Graham Nash had moved out six months earlier). He wrote "You Can Close Your Eyes" for Joni during this period. Linda Ronstadt, Carol King, and Carly Simon performed on his albums, and he often reciprocated.

Taylor met Simon when she first played at the Troubadour in 1971—instant Karma. A few months later they connected again when Taylor played at New York's Carnegie Hall. They married in November 1972. Both traveled to California for concerts, recording, or other business—but the transition back to the East Coast had begun. Taylor used the money from his early successful records to buy 175 acres of land on Martha's Vineyard and built a family house. They also bought a flat at 135 Central Park West in New York. Simon was an East Coast girl, and found California "un-Eastern". They wrote songs and sang about each other in the good times and the bad.

Through the rest of the 1970s, Taylor released 8 more albums, six of which ranked in Billboard's top 10. Singles such as "You've Got a Friend" and "How Sweet It Is (To Be Loved by You)" shot up to the top 5. Twice during the decade, he received a Grammy for best vocalist.

Simon also had an impressive string of hits. She recorded 8 successful studio albums in the 1970s, with "No Secrets" rising to #1 propelled by "You're so Vain" which was a #1 single. She had four other top-ten singles in the 1970s. She was one of the most successful female singer-songwriters of the decade. They became the Royal Couple of Rock n' Roll in the 1970s.

And then they weren't. They divorced in 1983. The pressures of two careers, Taylor's drug problems, and raising a family with two children became too much. The house on Martha's Vineyard was deeded to Simon and she still lives there today. Both continued their successful careers. Paul McCartney inducted Taylor into the Rock and Roll Hall of Fame in 2000; Simon was inducted into the Grammy Hall of Fame in 2004. Oh, and if you are still wondering, in 2015 Simon confessed that "You're so Vain" was about Warren Beatty. One of her LA memories.

Three Dog Night

In August 1967, three struggling singers who were Sunset Strip regulars decided to form a band. Danny Hutton convinced Cory Wells to join him, and then they recruited Chuck Negron another LA singer. Legend has it that they struggled to find a name for the band until Hutton's girlfriend suggested it after reading about how Australian dingoes keep warm. On very cold nights three dogs huddle together to share their body warmth. Thus *Three Dog Night* was born. Then they searched for musicians to fill out the band.

This band had complex ties to Laurel Canyon. Several had performed at the Troubadour before *Three Dog Night* was formed. Their style was built on the *Byrds* folk-rock sound. Hutton lived in the Canyon and still does. However, *3DN* also differed from the style of other Laurel Canyon bands. First, they were not typical singer/songwriters; they wrote very few of their successful records. Second, they focused on building a band that would be successful, rather than a band of friends. For example, the musicians in the band were capable of album recordings, while many other bands needed studio musicians. And when one musician left, they were replaceable. Under Hutton's leadership, it was more like a business than a collective of creative artists.

The next step was a record contract. Their manager arranged for the band to play at a Dunhill press party at the Whiskey, which led to a contract with Dunhill. The company was anxious to have an album on the market, and "Three Dog Night" was released in October 1968. It consisted entirely of other people's songs but played in a new and beautiful way. If *3DN* found a song that fit their goals, they played it.

The album shot up to #11 on the Billboard chart, and the top single "One" reached #1. The band was on the road to mega success. They went out touring to build support for the album. When they returned to LA they were the headliners at the Whiskey. Fame and fortune took less than a year.

Their music increased in popularity. Between 1969 and 1974 they had 20 consecutive top 50 hits on the Billboard charts, including 9 in the top 5, such as "Joy to the World" and "Celebrate". They also had 8 albums in Billboard's top 30.

Their success came because they selected songs from some of the best songwriters of the era (Lennon-McCartney, Randy Newman, Harry Nilson, Hoyt Axton, Sam Cook, Laura Nyro, Neil Young, and others). Then they developed an original sound with their unique harmonies and instrumentation.

At the same time, they began to over-celebrate their success, often at Hutton's party house at 2437 Horseshoe Canyon Road. Brian Wilson, some of the *Beatles,* and other famous artists would join them for the drugs and groupies. It became notorious in a Canyon full of notoriety. Their trajectory followed a familiar path. Negron, a long-time drug abuser, was arrested for possession of narcotics before the 1975 tour. Danny Hutton had an equally severe drug problem, and after the 1975 tour, he was thrown out of the band he formed. *3DN* never had a top 50 record or album after 1975, but Negron still performs at nostalgia concerts of the 1960s-1970s bands.

[Hutton House on Horseshoe Canyon Rd.]

***

Other artists—from Jimi Hendrix to Lara Nyro to Iggy Pop—passed through the Canyon during the decade. However, the mystique of Laurel Canyon was evaporating by the end of the 1970s. Even the second-wave artists were moving on. If they were successful, they moved west to Beverly Hills, Bel Air, Brentwood, or Malibu. If they weren't successful, they couldn't afford the escalating costs as executives and business types moved into the Canyon. Too many died of drug overdoses. There were still a few amazing moments in LA, like Christmas in 1977 when Carly Simon, James Taylor, Joni Mitchell, and James Brown decided to walk along Santa Monica Blvd. singing Christmas carols. But these moments became rarer and rarer.

8. MOTOWN MOVES TO LA

In the 1960s, Berry Gordy built a music empire in Detroit. Drawing upon historic African-American rhythm and blues traditions, Motown developed a distinct new sound. It was the sound of young Black America in the 1960s, represented by the *Miracles*, the *Supremes*, Marvin Gaye, the *Ronettes*, the *Four Tops*, the *Marvelettes*, the *Temptations*, *Martha and the Vandellas*, *Gladys Knight & the Pips*, Stevie Wonder, and more.

Berry Gordy founded Motown Records in April 1960. He scoured the region for singers and groups that matched his image for the label, and then molded them into the Motown Sound. This included classes on singing, etiquette, and wardrobe. He recorded Motown-written music in his Hitsville USA studio or other Motown studios. Then he marketed the music on the Motown label. From 1961 to 1971, Motown had 110 top-10 hits.

In the 1960s, Motown was popular in Los Angeles among African Americans and white youth. It was hip, it was powerful and intensely danceable. *Smokey Robinson and The Miracles* headlined at the Whisky a Go Go in January 1967. In March it was *The Temptations* and *Gladys Knight and the Pips*. *The Four Tops* in May 1967. Yet these were imports from Detroit rather than LA groups.

This changed in 1972 as Gordy moved Motown to its new headquarters at 6522 Sunset Blvd., Hollywood, California. Gordy had moved there earlier to prepare for the move. Some artists accompanied him to LA and some chose to stay in Detroit. Smokey Robinson moved West, as an artist and as vice president of Motown. A new era of Motown began, trying to repeat previous music success as well as connect to the movie and television worlds of Hollywood.

Diana Ross

Diana Ross was the star in Gordy's Motown heaven. She grew up in the Detroit projects with Mary Wilson and Florence Ballard. They persistently pressed Gordy until he signed them with Motown in 1961 (when they were high school juniors). The *Supremes'* 1964 single, "Where Did Our Love Go" launched their success, followed by 12 other #1 singles over the decade. Songs like "Stop! In the Name of Love", "Back in My Arms Again", "I Hear a Symphony" and "Love Child" cemented their status as Motown's top female voices with Ross as the lead.

Gordy and Diana Ross moved to California together in 1970 and he leased a house for her near his own. This was two years before Gordy moved Motown's HQ to Hollywood. Her solo career for Motown West continued her earlier success. "I Want You Back" topped the Billboard Hot 100 in January 1970. Of the two dozen singles she produced in the 1970s, half rose to the top 30 on the Billboard chart. After she married an LA businessman in 1971, she moved to Beverly Hills (701 Maple Dr.).

Part of the reason for Gordy, Motown, and Ross moving to Los Angeles was to make Ross a movie star. Motown Productions, the film and TV arm of Motown Records, produced the 1972 movie "Lady Sings the Blues" which brought critical acclaim.

[Diana Ross on Maple Drive, BH]

In her first movie, Ross received an Oscar nomination and a Golden Globe award for her portrayal of Billie Holiday. Two more Motown films, "Mahogany" (1975) and "The Wiz" (1978) followed, with Diana playing Dorothy in the remake of "The *Wizard of Oz*".

By the end of the decade, Diana Ross was an international celebrity as well as a famous Motown singer. She had borne Gordy's child, married another partner, and then divorced him. It was time to leave the past behind. She ended her contract with Motown in 1980 and moved back to New York City. In 1982, she became a permanent part of LA with a star on the Hollywood Walk of Fame (6712 Hollywood Blvd.)

Marvin Gaye

Marvin Gaye signed his first contract with Motown in 1960. Berry Gordy described his voice as "pure, mellow, soulful, and honest." Gaye worked his way up the Motown ladder, performing as a background musician and writing his own songs. Gaye married Berry Gordy's sister in 1964, and formally became part of the Motown family.

His recording career started picking up steam in 1964. Then came his single "How Sweet It Is (To Be Loved by You)" which reached the top 10. In 1966 "I Heard It Through the Grapevine" became Gaye's first single to reach #1. He was also known for his duets with female Motown signers from Mary Wells to Diana Ross. His soulful performances earned him the nickname of the "Prince of Motown".

Gaye's success was partly due to the unique quality of his voice, but he also developed a unique style that combined the soulfulness of gospel music, the sweetness of soft-soul pop, and the vocal skills of a jazz singer. After a break from his music, he returned to Motown in 1970.

Gaye was among the last of the Motown principals to move to Los Angeles. He eventually settled in a beautiful Hollywood Hills house (2737 Outpost Dr.) just off Mulholland Drive. Gaye lived here until his divorce in 1977. A subsequent renovation has created a mini-mansion.

[Gaye House on Outpost Dr.,]

In 1971 Motown released the controversial "What's Going On" which was Gaye's response to the racial and political violence of the day; it shot up to the top of the charts. During the decade he had 11 singles that reached the top 10 on the R&B chart. He released 5 albums during the 1970s, and all of them rose to the top 20 on the R&B chart. Toward the end of the decade,

Mother, mother
There's too many of you crying
Brother, brother, brother
There's far too many of you dying
You know we've got to find a way
To bring some lovin' here today, yeah

however, his career began to fade. One factor was his divorce in 1977, which was accompanied by new financial difficulties. Addiction problems added to the mix. Public tastes were also changing. Gaye even tried to record disco music to revive his career. The story doesn't end well.

[Gaye's Parents' House on. Gramercy Place, LA]

In 1975, Gaye's production company bought a beautiful old Craftsman house in West Adams (2101 S. Gramercy Place, LA) for Gaye's parents. Sadly, Gaye continued to struggle with drugs and financial problems. He returned from a tour and moved into his parents' house. During a family argument the senior Mr. Gaye, who was a Pentecostal minister, fatally shot his son on April 1st, 1984. Another good life trajectory came to the end. In his memory, Stevie Wonder wrote "Lighting Up the Candle" and sang it at Gaye's funeral. A year after his death, Motown produced a tribute album in his memory; "Motown Remembers Marvin Gaye". Track 1 was "I Heard It Through the Grapevine."

Stevie Wonder

In 1962 Berry Gordy heard twelve-year-old Seveland Morris sing and then quickly signed him to a Motown contract. The renamed Stevie Wonder had his first #1 hit a year later, "Fingertip—Part 2", and launched his career as part of the Motown family with songs, tours, and performances guided by Motown. During the rest of the 1960s, he steadily released new songs, including four more top 5 hits that reflected the Motown sound: "Uptight (Everything's Alright)", "I Was Made to Love Her", "For Once in My Life", and "My Cherie Amour".

The big change came on his 21st birthday when his contract with Motown expired in 1971. After nearly a decade of performing, Wonder wanted to take control of his career by writing and producing his music. He headed east to the Electric Lady Studios in New York which gave him access to a new music synthesizer (TONTO) and a new style. This produced a burst of creativity that spanned the rest of the decade. He started "Superstition" in NYC and then returned to the Crystal Studios in LA (1014 N. Vine, Hollywood) to produce the final version. It became his first #1 song since "Fingertip", demonstrating his new funky style using a Clavinet and the synthesizer.

This wasn't Wonder's first visit to LA. In 1963-64, Berry Gordy arranged for him to appear in two movies. Not the movies you would imagine. They starred Frankie Avalon and Annette Funicello: "Muscle Beach Party", "Bikini Beach", and an album derived from the movies, "Stevie at the Beach". Girls in bikinis, former Mouseketeers, and Stevie didn't mix well. Hopefully, his new move to LA would go better.

[Crystal Studios in LA]

He rejoined Motown on new terms that gave him creative freedom. Most of the songs in his albums "Talking Book" and "Innervisions" were produced in the Crystal Studios using equipment and producers from New York. This included another signature Wonder song, "You Are the Sunshine of My Life" that reached #1.

Wonder brought his technology with him to Record Plant (1032 N. Sycamore, LA) where most of the production occurred for three albums: "Fulfillingness," "Journey Through the Secret Life of Pets" and "Songs in the Key of Life" (also where the *Eagles* recorded "Hotel California"). Between 1972 and

[Record Plant Recording Studios]

1980, Wonder recorded six albums, all of which rose to the top 5 on the charts. Two of the albums reached #1 and cemented his stardom.

Wonder began using his celebrity for social causes. He lobbied Congress to name a national holiday for Martin Luther King. He was active in the fight against apartheid in South Africa, and raised funds for AIDS research and children and cancer charities. In 1984, he and Michael Jackson co-wrote "We are the World" for the USA Aid for Africa record. They assembled an all-star team of artists at A&M Recording Studios in the former

Charlie Chaplin Studios (1416 N. La Brea, LA). This later became the Jim Henson Studio, with Kermit greeting guests at the entrance.

Wonder's phenomenal career includes selling more than 100 million records with ten # 1 hits. He was nominated for 73 Grammy awards and won 25, as well as an Oscar for best song. He was inducted into the Rock and Roll Hall of Fame in 1989 by Paul Simon; the youngest inductee in the Hall's history. In 2009, President Obama awarded him the Gershwin Prize in popular music. Wonder has been an LA resident since the mid-1970s, owning homes in the Hollywood Hills and then Beverly Hills. He now lives in Los Angeles on Weybridge Ln. in the gated community of Bel-Air Crest. And every year he hosts a concert to provide toys for needy children in LA. His giving never stops.

The Jackson 5

In March 1969, Motown signed a new group of five brothers, *The Jackson 5* (Jackie, Tito, Jermaine, Marlon, and Michael). After signing, Gordy sent them to California to polish their performance with Motown's LA branch. Their first house in Los Angeles was in West Hollywood (1601 Queens Rd.). A huge change from the small family home they left behind in Gary, Indiana. Then Gordy leased them a bigger house in Beverly Hills.

The *Jackson 5* debuted on the Motown label with "I Want You Back" in October 1969; it topped the chart by January.

In 1971, after neighbors complained about the music "noise", the Jacksons moved to 4641 Hayvenhurst in Encino. It became the family compound for the next several decades. Michael lived in this house until he bought his Neverland estate in 1988.

Motown leveraged one artist with another. The *J5's* first album in 1969 was titled "Diana Ross Presents the Jackson 5". Jacksonmania began to build as they went on a national tour. The group had four consecutive #1 hits on the Billboard chart and young Michael was becoming a star before he reached his teens.

By the mid-1970s, however, the Motown magic began to fade. The *Four Tops, Gladys Knight and the Pips, The Temptations*, and others left the label. The renamed *Jacksons*, adding Janet and La Toya, continued to perform well on the R&B charts but national sales declined. There were strong bonds to Motown because it gave the group its start, and Jermaine was married to Gordy's daughter. Nevertheless, the *Jacksons* (minus Jermaine) decided to leave Motown and move to CBS records in 1975.

At the same time, Michael launched his solo career that had started under the Motown label. The adult Michael drew upon his creativity. In 1978 he played the Scarecrow in the Motown movie, "The Wiz", co-starring with Diana Ross. He began to write his music, and not just perform. His first album with CBS/Epix rose to #3 on the charts; the next five all rose to #1. The 1982 "Thriller" album became the best-selling album of its time, won 8 Grammys, and spent almost nine months at #1. Jackson's "Thriller" video premiered on MTV in December 1983 and transformed the medium. Michael became the "King of Pop" The Thriller house is located at 1345 Carroll Ave. in Los Angeles.

After going their own way, the *Jackson 5* sang together again in 1982 at the Pasadena Civic Center for a TV special celebrating Motown's 25th anniversary. One of the themes was the reunion of former groups: *Smokey Robinson and the Miracles, Diana Ross and the Supremes, The Four Tops, and The Temptations*. The high point of the night was the *Jackson 5* performing together again. After their performance, the other brothers left the stage and Michael sang "Billie Jean". This is the first time the world saw his famous

moonwalk. The night was a testament to what Berry Gordy had accomplished with his Motown label. The brothers did the "Victory" tour together in 1984, and then performed together once more in Madison Square Garden on September 10, 2001—they woke up the next morning to witness the terrorist attack on the Trade Center. Diana Ross inducted the *Jackson 5* into the Rock and Roll

Hall of Fame in 1997, with all the family attending. Michael's solo career was recognized in 2001, inducted by N*Sync.

Michael was a global multi-media star who experienced incredible success and difficult struggles over the subsequent decades. In June 2009 he began practicing at the LA Staples Center for his upcoming "This Is It" international tour. He stayed in a rented house in the Holmby Hills west of Beverly Hills (100 N Carolwood Dr.). After an exhausting rehearsal, he died on June 25th of cardiac arrest after receiving a propofol overdose at the house.

[Jackson's Death at N Carolwood Dr., Holmby Hills]

Smokey Robinson and Queen Latifah gave the eulogies for Jackson's memorial service at the Staples Center in July. Usher performed Jackson's "Gone Too Soon" as a tribute to Michael. He is buried at Forest Lawn Memorial Park's Hall of Liberty in the Hollywood Hills.

The Commodores and Lionel Richie

In 1968, a group of Tuskegee Institute students formed a band and began playing locally in Alabama. After continuing arguments about a name, they let fate decide. They opened a dictionary to a random page, and then randomly selected a word on the page—the *Commodores* were born.

Two years later they auditioned in New York City and won a job as the opening act on the *Jackson 5* tours in 1970 and 1971. They were one of the last groups to sign with Motown in 1972. This began their training at Motown University (while still taking Tuskegee classes toward their college degrees). The Motown system taught them about the intricacies of writing and performing, the details of recording, and touring with other Motown artists. The *Commodores* also brought something new, a fusion of funk, soul, and rock that was missing from Motown's label.

As other Motown groups peaked or disbanded, the *Commodores* were moving up as part of Motown West. Their second album, "Caught in the Act" was their first to break into the top 30 on the pop chart and #7 on R&B. Their next album "Commodores" spent eight weeks at the top of the R&B chart. They built their fan base by touring with the Rolling Stones and then their own US and international tours.

Lionel Richie started writing more and singing more, featured in many of their most popular new songs. Richie also moved their style away from funk toward pop songs that would have cross-over appeal and more sales. Their fifth studio album rewarded this strategy with seven weeks at the top of the R&B chart and #3 on the pop chart. Songs like "Just to Be Close to You", "Easy", and "Three Times a Lady" created an identity for Richie's style and made the *Commodores* one of the mainstays of the Motown collection. Their 1979 single, "Still" was Richie's last #1 hit with the group. During the 1970s, the *Commodores* had 8 songs in the top 25 of the pop chart, and 14 on the top 25 R&B chart. They were one of Motown's most successful male groups by the end of the decade, and a reconstituted group still tours today.

"Lionel Richie" in 1982 was his first solo album. In 1983, with Motown's support, Richie pursued a solo career. He offered a softer style of ballads featuring his distinct voice. His songs found a wide audience, generating 13 straight top 10 singles in the 1980s. One of Richie's most memorable performances was as the headliner for the closing ceremonies of the 1984 Olympics in Los Angeles. In 1984, he and Michael Jackson co-wrote "We are the World" for the USA Aid for Africa record. He's won four Grammys, a Golden Globe, and an Oscar. His career appears never-ending. Today Richie lives in a magnificent 28-room mansion in Beverly Hills, overlooking the fourth hole of the LA Country Club (145 Copley Pl.). It all began with Berry Gordy enabling a group of young black college students to develop their musical dreams.

* * *

The real success story of Motown should focus on the Detroit years when Gordy created a top-down music factory that produced some of the most memorable artists and sounds of contemporary music. At its peak, Motown was the largest black-owned business in America. Still, the last chapters of the Motown story occurred in LA. Fittingly, the Grammy's celebrated the 60th anniversary of Motown at LA Live in February 2019. It was a bittersweet night. On the one hand, the nostalgia ran deep as Diana Ross, Smokey Robinson, and Stevie Wonder performed, with many former Motown employees and one of this book's authors in the audience. On the other hand, most of the artists who made Motown successful are no longer alive. Berry Gordy was there in the first row—alive and well and enjoying the celebration.

9. BEYOND ROCK N'ROLL – HARD ROCK MADE IN CALIFORNIA

Rock n'Roll in the 1960s-1970s developed into hard rock and eventually heavy metal. Although these developments did not predominantly appear under the Southern California sun, some of them can be linked to the West Coast. One of the foundational moments of hard rock – for some it even represents a foundational moment of heavy metal – is part of LA history. In 1968 the *Beatles* wanted to make a song that was noisier than any other song, and in particular any song by *The Who*. Paul McCartney wrote "Helter Skelter", included in the chef d'oeuvre "The White Album". Charles Manson was convinced that this song contained a hidden message, some sort of prophecy about a racial war in which the Manson Family would become a world-saving group of white supremacists. In August 1969, Manson and four of The Family's members entered 3301 Waverly Drive, the home of Leno and Rosemary LaBianca. After brutally murdering the couple, they left several messages behind. Patricia Krenwinkel, one of the killers, wrote (and misspelled) HEALTER SKELTER with Rosemary's blood on the LaBianca's fridge.

For Manson, the *Beatles'* recordings contained hidden subliminal messages. Indeed, the *Beatles* innovated in their 1966 album "Revolver" with novel artistic "backmasking". Backmasking means that the message can only be heard by playing the record backward. With the development of CDs, controversies about backmasking became more or less obsolete. "Helter Skelter", however, is one of the most covered Beatles songs ever.

Music-wise, the link between Southern California and hard rock was rather weak. It predominately came about through British bands, such as *Led Zeppelin*, *The Who*, *Deep Purple*, or *Queen*. In the US, important hard rock bands emerged on the East Coast, such as *KISS* or *Aerosmith*. Others came from down under, most importantly the Australian band *AC/DC*. There are four California exceptions, however: *Iron Butterfly* from San Diego, *Steppenwolf* (an LA spin-off from a Canadian band), *Van Halen* (from Pasadena), and *Metallica* (from LA).

Formed in 1966, *Iron Butterfly* landed a top-30 hit with their "In-A-Gadda-Da-Vida". The track lasted for over 17 minutes and its success gave *Iron Butterfly* a booking for Woodstock in August 1969. However, the band got stuck in New York's LaGuardia Airport. When they asked for a helicopter to take them to Woodstock and back, Woodstock Production Coordinator John Morris sent a telegram to the band. The first letter of each line in the telegram made it clear that *Iron Butterfly* should rather go home to California: (the telegram read: "**F**or reasons I can't go into / **U**ntil you are here / **C**larifying your situation / **K**nowing you are having problems / **Y**ou will have to find / **O**ther transportation / **U**nless you plan not to come.")

A book on road trips through SoCal has to mention *Steppenwolf*. Their song "Born to be Wild" and the epic film "Easy Rider" added Harley Davidsons – or any other bike – to the road trip experience. So here you go. Steppenwolf was founded in Los Angeles in 1967 by members of the Canadian band, *The Sparrows*. Their songs made the Billboard charts, and hits such as "The Pusher" and "Born to be Wild" were closely associated with road trips through the West, albeit on two rather than with four wheels. In the opening credits of the cult film "Easy Rider", the song "Born to be Wild" first mentions the term "heavy metal", referring to motorcycles, however:

I like smoke and lightnin'
Heavy metal thunder
Racing with the wind
And the feeling that I'm under

Another California band that profoundly shaped hard rock is undoubtedly *Van Halen*. Born in Amsterdam in the 1950s, the two brothers, Eddie and Alex, moved with their family to Pasadena in 1962 (881 Las Lunas St, Pasadena). They started a band with David Lee Roth as the lead singer. After several years of touring and Sunset Strip bookings, eventually getting pushed by Gene Simmons of *Kiss*, they got their first and only number-one hit in the US charts, "Jump", in 1984. That same year, Eddie Van Halen invented the innovative guitar technique called "tapping" which got him a guitar solo in Michael Jackson's "Beat It".

To finish the SoCal's hard rock/heavy metal history, one has to mention *Metallica*. The band was formed in Los Angeles in 1981. It is the only band mentioned in this chapter that still performs and is at its very top. Their 11th studio album is in the making. *Metallica* is primarily based in San Francisco and is one of the most commercially successful bands of all time. One of this book's authors saw them in concert in Austin's Zilker Park in 2018 – where, by the way, Paul McCartney also performed.

Californian hard rock/heavy metal history should not forget the typically LA-type progressive rock promoted by bands such as *TOTO*. This band's history can be traced back to a garage in the Valley (13608 Valleyheart Dr., Sherman Oaks)—home of the Porcaro family.

In the Pocaros's garage, numerous legendary musicians got together from the 1970s onwards. The "pater familias", Joe Porcaro, was a jazz drummer who recorded with *The Monkees*, *Pink Floyd*, Frank Sinatra, Madonna, and others. He is, however, better known as the father of three boys who started a band out of their famous garage in 1977. The Porcaro boys were students at Grant High School, where they met David Paich and Steve Lukather, to form *TOTO*. [Fun fact: Tom Selleck went to that same school, but went for helicopter-flying and Ferrari-driving gigs in Hawaii instead of becoming a professional musician]. *TOTO* became one of the best-selling music groups of the era, combining

many different musical styles and leaving a firm fingerprint on the music scene in California – and beyond. Even without thinking of climate change, their song "Africa" about the rain that falls on Africa became an iconic image. *TOTO* is distinguished from most bands by their unparalleled instrumental skills. Yes, Eddie Van Halen provided the guitar solo in Jackson's "Beat it". But the rest of the track is basically a *TOTO* song. Steve Lukather played both lead guitar and bass guitar on that track, Steve Porcaro was on synthesizers, and Jeff Porcaro on drums. And regarding Van Halen's iconic guitar solo, Steve Lukather had to "smooth" the track a bit. Forty years later, *TOTO* still tours, despite having been hit by some kind of curse: Jeff Porcaro, arguably one of the best rock drummers ever, mysteriously died in 1992, apparently from inhaling pesticides while gardening. Bass player and brother of Jeff, Mike Porcaro, was diagnosed with Amyotrophic lateral sclerosis (ALS) in 2010 and succumbed to this hideous illness in 2015.

Not just with the members of *TOTO*, Los Angeles is one of the greatest places on earth to find rock session musicians, or studio musicians as they are sometimes called. Some session musicians got together in band-like formations and became known in their own right. Most notably, the *Wrecking Crew* whose members had solid backgrounds in jazz and classical music, before becoming associated with Phil Spector. The *Wrecking Crew* worked with many of the artists mentioned in this book, such as the *Beach Boys* and *Sonny & Cher*. With Motown's move to Los Angeles in 1972, however, one of the most successful session musician formations, the *Funk Brothers*, dissolved. California was not the promised land for everybody.

In 1985, Los Angeles saw the birth of a less soft, but just as commercial band that became one of the best-selling hard rock bands ever: *Guns N' Roses*. Their debut album "Appetite for Destruction" eventually became the USA's best-selling debut album. Lead singer Axl Rose, guitarist Slash, and their fellow band members broke another record in 2008. Their album "Chinese Democracy" became the most expensive rock album ever produced. However, the bold move to combine China with Democracy did not lead to the anticipated success. When not on tour, Axl Rose lives high in a Malibu canyon overlooking the Pacific Ocean.

Much more could be written about the legacy of these California-based artists who changed the world of music. But our road trip comes to an end, as every road trip eventually does. For many of these prodigies under the West Coast sun, the trip ended too early. In the 1960s and 1970s, rock stars tended to die of stimulant drugs and opiate overdoses. California-grown rock stars of the 1980s rather died of gardening (Jeff Porcaro), sedation drugs (Michael Jackson), alcoholism and cancer (Eddie Van Halen), and ALS (Mike Porcaro). Gladly, some of them are still alive today – and you may run into them on your next road trip through Southern California (e.g., David Lee Roth, James Hetfield, Steve Lukather, David Paich, John Kay, and even Paul McCartney and Ringo Starr).

SOURCES

Beatlebible.com

Mark Bego, *Cher: If You Believe*. New York: Cooper Square Press, 2001.

Cher, *The First Time*. New York: Simon and Schuster, 1998.

Peter Carlin, *Catch a Wave: The Rise, Fall, and Redemption of the Beach Boys' Brian Wilson*. Emmaus, PA: Rodale, 2006.

Judy Collins, *Sweet Judy Blue Eyes: My Life in Music*. New York: Crown, 2011.

Sharon Davis, *Lionel Richie: Hello*. London: Equinox, 2009.

Stephen Davis, *Jim Morrison: Life, Death, Legend*. New York: Gotham Books, 2004.

Stephen Davis, *More Room in a Broken Heart: The True Adventures of Carly Simon*. New York: Gotham Books, 2012.

Micky Dolenz, *I'm a Believer: My life of Monkees, Music, and Madness*. New York: Hyperion, 1993.

Michael Dyson, *Mercy Mercy Me: The Art, Loves, and Demons of Marvin Gaye*. New York: Civitas Books, 2008.

Michael Farber, *Laurel Canyon: The Inside Story of Rock and Roll's Legendary Neighborhood*. New York: Faber and Faber, 2006.

Eddie Fiegel, *Dream a Little Dream of Me: The Life of 'Mama Cass Elliot*. London: Pan Macmillan, 2005.

Michael Heatley, *Neil Young: His Life and Music*. London: Hamlin, 1994.

Barney Hoskins, *Hotel California*. Hoboken, NJ: John Wiley, 2006.

Jermaine Jackson, *You Are Not Alone. Michael: Through a Brother's Eyes*. New York: Simon and Schuster, 2011.

Katherine Monk, *Joni: The Creative Odyssey of Joni Mitchell*. Berkeley, CA: Greystone Books, 2012.

Philip Norman, *John Lennon: The Life*. New York: HarperCollins, 2008.

Mark Ribowsky, *Signed, Sealed, and Delivered: The Soulful Journey of Stevie Wonder*. New York: Wiley, 2010.

Linda Ronstadt, *Simple Dreams: A Musical Memoir*. New York: Simon and Schuster, 2013.

Diana Ross, *Memoirs: Secrets of a Sparrow*. New York: Villard, 1993.

Dean Torrence, *Surf City: The Jan & Dean Story*. 2016.

Sheila Weller, *Girls Like Us: Carole King, Joni Mitchell, and Carly Simon--and the journey of a generation*. New York: Atria Books, 2008.

Timothy White, *The Nearest Faraway Place: Brian Wilson, The Beach Boys, and the Southern California Experience*. New York: Henry Holt, 1994.

Timothy White, *James Taylor: Long Ago and Far Away*. Omnibus Press, 2002.

ABOUT THE AUTHORS

Russell Dalton grew up in Southern California in the 1960s. He drove his 1959 Corvette to the A&W in Hawthorne, spent weekends on the Sunset Strip, and played guitar. His goal in high school was to be in a rock band or join the U.S. Foreign Service. Unfortunately, he couldn't sing and his ability to play instruments was equally limited. So he followed a life course that led to the U.S. foreign service in 1976. After completing his Ph.D., he became a college professor at Florida State University and then the University of California, Irvine.

Diego Garzia was born in Southern California way before he was actually born. He grew up with a left-handed Stratocaster at home but never managed to realize the difference. Considering his equally weak singing skills, he hijacked numerous bands all over the world to be the lead drummer. He pursued an honest academic career until he realized that his people were on the Venice boardwalk instead. Since then, he tries to find his way out of the business. He is currently teaching political science research methods on Zoom at the University of Lausanne.

Alexander H. Trechsel grew up in Switzerland, with a two-year interlude as a toddler in Tucson, AZ. There his parents drove him around in a red, 1960s Mustang. His love for classical music was stronger than his pianistic skills, but by joining numerous rock bands and eventually declaring himself a lead singer, he successfully camouflaged his musical deficits. He studied politics in Geneva, before teaching at the European University Institute in Florence for over a decade. In 2016, he moved back to Switzerland and now works at the University of Lucerne.

Printed in Great Britain
by Amazon